GAIJIN LIVE NEXT DOOR

EIGHT YEARS IN JAPAN

HEATHER HACKETT

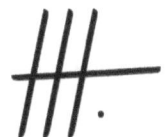

First Edition June 2020

ISBN: 978-0-6480093-1-3

Copyright © 2019 by Heather Hackett

All rights reserved.

No part of this book may be reproduced in any form or by any electronic or mechanical means, including information storage and retrieval systems, without the prior written permission of the author, except in the case of brief quotations embodied in a book review and certain other non-commercial uses permitted by copyright law.

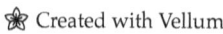 Created with Vellum

For Mani and Noa

My two bright shining lights

Gaijin Live Next Door

is the second book in the
Ten Years From Home memoir series.

It continues the stories of our travels contained in

RESTLESS: MEMOIR OF AN INCURABLE TRAVELLER

Pick up your copy from Amazon
https://www.amazon.com/dp/B01MXSWC3J

1984

1

TIME OUT

Coming home to Australia after 12 months overseas was a shock. After so long on the crowded, narrow streets and alleyways of Asia, I couldn't help thinking that my hometown had been flattened by a nuclear blast during our absence. And crossing streets that seemed almost wide enough to land an aircraft took some getting used to. The low-rise buildings contrasted sharply with the soaring skyscrapers of the teeming cities we had only recently departed and lent credence to the illusion that the world was indeed flat.

Our families got quite a shock when they discovered I was already six months pregnant. They greeted us with, "You should have told us!" But the overwhelming flurry of concern my 'condition' gave rise to made me suspect the decision to keep it quiet had been the right one. Our families exposed themselves as an army of professional worriers.

As we began to plan for the homebirth of our first child, keeping quiet became the rule of the day. The general consensus was that no one in their right mind should consider giving birth at home, especially not with their first. Initially, I argued, pointing out that up until recently most births occurred at home. Hell, even our own parents and their siblings had been born at home. But it carried no weight, only more cynicism. I was regaled with tales of all that could go wrong, even by the family doctor, especially by the family doctor, who, after hearing of the lack of food I had suffered through in China, informed me my baby was too small for the dates I had given him. (Mani weighed almost four kilos at birth.) So, I found another doctor, one who was willing to see a first-time mum with a dogged determination to be treated like a human being, and not just a patient with a condition.

I was berated for rejecting the modern technology that the omnipresent 'they' had worked so hard for. "Get yourself up to the hospital where you belong so we can all visit you!" What the…! You mean, if I have my baby at home where there are no restrictions on visiting hours or when you can and can't see the baby, you won't come visit? Some weird kind of logic at play there. So, I shut my mouth and quietly went about preparing for a home birth.

Everything 'at home' had changed. Nothing about it was as I remembered. Not the town, not the people, not the life I used to live. It's strange to feel culture shock in your own country, in a place you have called home. It's like a slap in the face that wakes you from a momentary stupor. I knew it had been my choice to leave the country, and life had continued as normal without me, but no one was particularly interested in what had happened to me, to us. The stories we had lived were so far removed from small, country town life that people couldn't relate to them. Or to James and me. It made me feel as though our experiences didn't count, weren't real, had no value, that the trip had been just a minor blip in our lives; like we'd gone off the rails for a while, but now we had to face reality. Now that we were having a child, we were expected to knuckle down and 'resume normal operation'.

And just like that I came to realize that the thing that had changed the most about my life was me.

It's a peculiar thing, but if I hadn't come home, I might not have known that for a much longer time. I had grown up kowtowing to authority, staying silent in the face of conflict; but after a year on the road, I had become more confident. I was more accustomed to fighting for my rights — a bed in a Chinese hotel dormitory, or a sleeping berth on a crowded train. And being pregnant made me even more determined. I refused to accept shit just because that was all that was on offer. It was strangely satisfying, yet simultaneously disappointing. There was an invisible wedge hammering its way between me and all I had once held dear.

The pressure to conform was enormous. Even my clothes were deemed strange, and I was strange because of them. Once, Mum crossed the street to avoid having to meet me in public because of how I was dressed. And Dad refused to let me take the mattress from my old room because I didn't want the entire ensemble and intended to lay it on the floor.

Our little flat in the suburbs lacked any furniture apart from one old bean bag chair and some cushions and rugs. Everyone knew that we were flat broke after our year away, and that wouldn't have been so bad in their eyes except that we appeared not to care. Apparently, that was weird, wrong even. It wasn't how I was raised, and hence, unfathomable.

We had isolated ourselves by doing something different. Yet, in the places where we had spent the last 12 months, it wasn't different at all. It was the way it was — normal. We started to question where we truly belonged, and why we felt more at ease among strangers. And foreigners.

As the date of Mani's birth approached, we decided to undertake a ten-day course in Vipassana[1] meditation as suggested by a random stranger on the India/Nepal border. It would mean living a simple life for that time, following the five Buddhist precepts:

- No killing — hence a vegan diet
- No taking what is not given
- No sexual misconduct — or contact of any kind with the opposite sex

- No taking intoxicating substances e.g. drugs, either illegal or legal, such as medication, tobacco, and alcohol
- No lying or gossiping — actually, no speaking at all, except to ask questions of the teacher. Buddhists call it Noble Silence – quiet throughout one's whole being.

My family disparaged this plan as an impossible task, but I welcomed the opportunity. Peace and uninterrupted quiet. Not having to talk to anyone or to justify anything. Bliss. Of course it would be challenging, especially in my advanced pregnant state, but all worthwhile things usually are. The hardest part for me was no writing, reading, or listening to music. Noble Silence. It sounded like a lofty goal, but I was determined to commit to the full experience. And I did.

By the end of the ten days, I felt I knew my co-meditators better than if we had been communicating all along. I had simply observed them. When the last day arrived and we were again free to speak, I knew whom I wanted to talk with. But it wasn't that easy. My first close encounter upon being given the green light to speak took place in the bathroom. I had no idea what to say, so I said nothing. The woman and I looked at each other, opened and closed our mouths a couple of times, then laughed. There was no need to say anything after all.

I'll never forget the parting words of the teacher who conducted that ten-day course, "Meditating is only the second hardest thing in the world to do. Not meditating is the hardest."

And so, on our return to our little flat in the suburbs, we put what we had learnt into practice, turning the spare bedroom into a meditation cell complete with cushions, candles and incense. For our families, it just confirmed what they had suspected all along — we were most certainly stark raving mad.

Mani's birth took place at home as planned, just three months after our return from overseas. It was another challenge, long and tiring, as every other mother on Earth knows. But it was natural, free of intervention, and safe. The doctor I had been seeing for the last trimester of my pregnancy asked if he could come to the birth as a friend rather than a doctor. It was still illegal back then for him to be present in any official capacity. By lunch time the next day, the bush telegraph had broadcast the controversial news of his attendance all over town.

Closer to home, everyone breathed a huge sigh of relief that we didn't both die, which had been the predicted outcome. I believe we were protected by two of life's beautiful ironies, the naivety of youth, and the belief that you are bulletproof.

The pressure didn't ease up following Mani's safe arrival. True to my hippie label, I refused to use a pacifier, a cot, or even a pram, opting instead for the bamboo cradle we had ferried all the way home from Burma and a front-fitting baby carrier we had purchased in Hong Kong. Nowadays, every man and his dog knows what a baby carrier is, but back then they were largely unheard of. And, by extrapolation, strange.

"You can't put a one-week-old baby in that thing!" my mother admonished just before our first foray into the world with a baby in tow. "You should have a pram!" Her emphasis on the word 'should' made it sound like a threat.

I remember the day clearly; it was pouring with rain, and the carrier would have been perfect to protect him from the weather and enable me to hold an umbrella with my free hands. But oh no, I caved in the face of her judgmental words, miserably failing at being the new, strong woman I thought I'd grown to be. How is it that mothers can sometimes do that, turn you into a little child all over again with just a few well-executed, critical words?

It was a horrendous experience for us all. Everyone got wet and assumed a depressing mood that matched the weather. The day went downhill fast, and we scurried home again without completing all the business we had on our list. And we didn't venture out again for a week.

If I was struggling to deal with the burden of being caught between my newfound freedom and our families' traditional values, James wasn't coping with it at all. When he suggested we move to Perth, I was torn. It was about as far away from 'home' as we could afford to go. It would certainly get us away from the pressure he was under to 'provide for his family', but at what cost? Perth was so far away. The other side of the country. Admittedly, I was growing tired of being caught in the crossfire, of having to defend my husband against my family, of having to justify what couldn't really be justified. I had a new baby. I didn't need any extraneous drama. But I had to choose a side, and there was clearly no choice. It was heart-breaking.

So, there we were, leaving home. Again. It only brought more despair to those closest to us. We had no money to travel overseas, and there wasn't much work to be had where we were. In 1984, unemployment rates in small country towns such as ours were at an all-time high. So, we moved to where the jobs were more plentiful, and the family ties less binding — to Perth, almost 4,000 kilometers away. And we got there by the cheapest means possible, a non-stop, 72-hour, cross-country bus service. Mani was just six weeks old.

The journey across the country from east to west was as uneventful as it was long. Three days, two rotating drivers, and only enough stops to pick up in Melbourne and Adelaide, and feed and water the passengers. An empty seat behind ours became home to Mani's bamboo cradle, and every time he stirred, I fed him, changed him, or brought him forward for a cuddle on our laps. He was so quiet that we were halfway across the desert before some of our fellow travelers even knew he was aboard. It wasn't until we reached Perth and began the search for accommodation that the true reality of traveling with a baby began to sink in.

It seems that all the world loves a baby, but no one wants to share their apartment building with one. Flats and apartments in the city were cheap enough, just $40-50 a week, and readily available, but convincing the gatekeepers that we were desirable tenants was an emotionally costly exercise. It wasn't until I actually broke down and started sobbing into the public phone receiver as I begged yet another stranger with an English accent to give us a chance that we even got to first base.

Gwen finally agreed to let us take a look at the cheap and nasty, semi-furnished apartment with vomit-green carpet that she and her husband Harry managed. It took us only five minutes in person to convince her that we were 'acceptable' tenants. She loved all three of us. It was such a relief I almost began crying all over again.

As it turned out, jobs weren't any easier to get in the west than they were in the east, unless you were looking to work in the mines on a fly-in-fly-out basis. So, we came up with the plan, a rather loose term, to go to Korea to make our fortunes as English teachers. We had heard the money was good and the visas relatively easy to get. That neither of us had any training as teachers of English as a foreign language or spoke even a word of Korean didn't deter us in the slightest. As I said before, young and bulletproof.

We spent the next few months hunkered down in the tiny flat, meditating, perfecting a vegetarian diet, and assisting Gwen and Harry with the day-to-day maintenance of the block of apartments. They had taken quite a shine to us, and by the time we left, they were our biggest fans. We spent a lot of time at the city library, borrowing and reading anything we could find on Asian culture. It helped us deal with our culture shock, made us feel like we were still traveling.

After just three months out west, we made the irksome trip back across the country, not quite as easy with a curious six-month-old. Back in Sydney, James did a hasty TEFL (Teaching English as a Foreign Language) course to lend some credibility to the English teacher status he was hoping to achieve. It was there, from his fellow students, James learned that the prospects for teaching English in South Korea had taken a turn for the worse. Jobs were hard to come by and working visas practically never granted. They told him Japan was a much less risky choice for prospective teachers of English. The downside was that it was horrendously expensive.

We decided to apply for working holiday visas for Japan, just in case the need arose, but having a baby included in your passport prevented one from being granted. The upshot was, James' application was approved and mine was not. I would have to make do with a three-month tourist visa if we ended up there.

To the dismay of friends and family who had assumed a baby would tie us down, we made the leap of faith that's always required when chasing dreams and left the country yet again.

Having been out of work for almost 12 months now, we were a little light on cash, but we'd managed to save enough for one-way tickets to Hong Kong. It had meant living like nomads with no social lives for most of that time, but the end somehow justified the means. We were both too busy being new hippie parents to worry about what went on outside our front door.

On departure, our only real plan was to purchase onward tickets in Hong Kong, where flights to anywhere were much cheaper than in Australia. We had no pre-booked accommodation, no knowledge of the language and no pre-arranged jobs to go to. We were just two adults, twenty-something adults, a nine-month-old baby and two backpacks bulging with cloth diapers.

This time we were gone for more than eight years.

1985

2

ARE WE JAPANESE OR ARE WE ALIENS?

*T*o say we were unprepared for Japan is an understatement of no small proportions. A few weeks before we arrived, we hadn't even been certain we were headed that way. The direction of our journey had turned toward the Land of the Rising Sun only after a chance meeting in a Chungking Mansions elevator in Hong Kong.

"Korea's no longer a go." Our fellow traveler confirmed what we had heard in Sydney. "They're cracking down. You need a degree at the very least, and jobs have dried up. But Japan is wide open." And with little more than that to go on, we bought one-way tickets to Tokyo instead of Seoul. Beyond that, we had no plan at all.

We landed at Narita International Airport in early April afternoon rain. As soon as we entered the arrivals hall, it was obvious we weren't in Kansas anymore. The signs directing inbound passengers were clear. Japanese this way, Aliens over there. We didn't seem to belong in either category. I didn't know whether to be mildly confused or profoundly offended, and I wondered exactly how I was going to answer the inevitable question, "Where are you from?" Should I launch into a long, convoluted explanation about how we were actually heading for Venus, but our spaceship had been thrown off course by the rings of Saturn and we were forced to drop out of warp speed and de-cloak just south of Jupiter? Maybe the flight from Hong Kong had taken us off-planet and this really wasn't Earth. Though I was unaware of it then, I would begin to believe this was in fact the case in about three hours' time.

Our dog-eared passports drew some suspicion at Immigration Control, overflowing as they were with illegible rubber stamp imprints from countless other Asian bureaucracies. It was hardly our fault that some of the countries we had recently visited liked to take up several valuable pages with their entry and exit stamps, or that the Australian Government refused to issue extra pages when passports were filled, even if they were still valid for two more years.

We didn't do much to impress the team at the customs desk either. After some heavy eyeballing of our scruffy backpacks and the baby on my back, there was a difficult conversation about where we would be staying, how long we planned to stay, the purpose of our visit to Japan, and how much money we had. It was difficult because we had no plan and no firm answers to those questions. Since James was arriving on a working holiday visa and Mani and I had only 90-day tourist visas, we must have appeared suspicious. In similar circumstances, I doubt two scruffy foreigners would have been allowed to enter Australia, but apparently, we satisfied the stern, uniformed agent who held our fate in his white-gloved hands, along with our bruised and battered passports. Some food items we were carrying were of greater concern.

Knowing it might be quite some time before we saw our beloved Vegemite again, I'd managed to squeeze a couple of small jars of my favorite toast topping into one of the packs, along with some caffeine-free drink powder and a box of breakfast cereal.

"You have banana?" The unsmiling customs officer pointed an accusatory finger at the picture of some sliced banana in a bowl of cereal that adorned the packet of cereal at the bottom of one of our bags. Like a dog following the scent of a bone, he'd had to dig a long way to find the one thing that could shoot down our entire trip.

What the...? Had he never seen a box of cereal before? It's not like it comes out of the box with fresh fruit and milk in place, ready to eat. James stumbled over the explanation, clearly worried that he wasn't making sense.

"No. It's just a serving suggestion. You have to add the banana. If you want. There is no banana. We have no banana." It was getting worse.

"No banana?"

"No! No banana!" James shook his head and waved his hands over the picture, as if the offending fruit would magically disappear. He tried a different tack. "Yes! No banana!"

"Okay. Enter this way." He dismissed us without making eye contact, though I noticed he watched in mild disgust as we crammed all our personal effects back into the bags whichever way they would fit. They no longer did. I had spent quite a bit of effort pre-flight rolling all our clothes into neat cylinders so that everything we needed got to accompany us on the journey. I wasn't happy, but I was also a bit scared. Airport arrival halls had a strange effect on me. I always suffered an incredible, and unwarranted, surge of guilt for some unnamed crime that would see me handcuffed and hauled away, never to be heard of again.

Armed with only a dog-eared and out of date copy of the Lonely Planet™ guide to Japan, we headed for the banks of public phones, conspicuous in their luminous, fluro-green covers. For the next six hours, James entertained Mani, and I shoveled coins into the slots like a crazed gambling addict, making phone call after phone call to potential accommodation venues.

But my pleas for a room for even one night fell on unsympathetic ears. Deja vu. It was Perth all over again, only more distressing. This was a whole other country, and one in which we knew no one, nor the language. I knew that it wasn't going to be a walk in the park, getting into Japan and setting up house; I guess I just didn't expect it to be this hard either. I thought I was tougher than this. I was wrong.

At first it was just a matter of every hostel being fully booked, but soon the real reason for the refusals came tumbling out — "We don't want any baby!"

I tried not to crumple, though inwardly I was crushed. My son was a quiet baby. He wasn't a crier. Fuck! We had traveled from one side of Australia to the other on a non-stop bloody bus when he was six weeks old and no one even knew he was there. I started to cry in frustration. I started to beg. That only made them angry. It wasn't until years later that I understood how 'un-Japanese' I had behaved; I had upset their *wa*.[1]

"Please! We have nowhere else to go. We're still at the airport. I don't know what else to do." My head was full of exclamation marks. It wasn't the first time that evening I had spoken to the guy on the other end of this call, but I wasn't making any headway. I knew he had a room because the first time I'd called, I didn't mention the baby until he had confirmed that he had availability. My subterfuge didn't work.

He started to lecture me. "I don't think much of your holiday planning. Japan is very expensive. If you don't have a plan, you will spend a lot of money here."

Holiday? I wanted to scream at him. We had arrived here to look for work and to start a new life with a nine-month-old baby and only the contents of two backpacks. We must surely be insane. It wasn't going to be a picnic, let alone a holiday. But he was more steadfast in his denial than I was at breaking down the walls he threw up. I was losing the will to live. And it was all starting to feel like a huge mistake. I hung up the receiver, having achieved nothing.

Completely disheartened now, I trudged back to the row of seats that looked destined to become our beds for the night and fell into one of the uncomfortable plastic chairs, tired, emotional, defeated, and thoroughly pissed. James and Mani were playing a game of peek-a-boo with one of the boarding passes.

"It's your turn," I said in a monotone. James looked at me blankly, as if he were unable to comprehend the fact that I still hadn't managed to find a room for the night. "I'm fucking over it!"

Though he didn't persist for as long as I had, he had no success either, and deemed it pointless. I had already called every guest house in the Greater Tokyo metropolitan area.

There was no other choice than to head over to the official hotel reservation counter with our tails between our legs, broken and defeated. I'd been on the phone almost continuously for over six hours, apart from crying breaks, and my fingers ached from alternately dialing numbers and wringing my hands in despair. The last train had long since left on its 60-kilometer journey to Tokyo Station, so the only remaining option was the Limousine Bus, a fancy name for an ordinary coach with blue velour seats and lights in the floor of the aisle.

It was a quiet, dejected, one-hour ride, just the three of us and the driver, on a dimly lit, luxury coach. I stared out the window as the orange neon lights of the freeway flashed past, mesmerized by them and the rain spattering the windows. Even the sky was crying. We arrived at Tokyo Station around midnight with a booking for a hotel on the Ginza with a price tag that we could not afford if our stay in Japan was going to last longer than a few days.

3

ONE DOOR CLOSES…

Tokyo Station is like a small city, with 3,000 trains and millions of passengers passing through it every day. But the last trains roll away from the platforms at midnight, so apart from a few old men wielding mops and brooms, it was largely deserted. Finding the right exit from the hundreds of options was a nightmare. There wasn't a single, helpful sign in English announcing, 'Ginza Hotels This Way', so we stumbled around in a daze for an interminable half hour. Like the guy on the phone, I was also starting to deplore our lack of planning. After wandering blindly, following our noses in no particular direction, we miraculously emerged into the cool, rainy night on the right side of the tracks, the Ginza side of the tracks.

Breaking our own golden rule of travel — never trust a local — by asking a local for help, an elderly gentleman waiting for a taxi pointed us in the direction of our hotel. This 'rule' was borne of our experience while traveling in other Asian countries; locals were either too helpful, insisting on accompanying us to our destination, or had no idea what we wanted but offered suggestions anyway. Either way, it rarely ended well. The man spoke a little English, enough to hurriedly advise us that it was a long way and suggested we should take a cab. In typical, stubborn Aussie style, after confirming the correct direction, we set off on foot. In the rain. Without umbrellas.

Fifteen minutes later, stinking of green public phones and sanitized velour upholstery, we stumbled into the marble lobby of a four-star hotel in Tokyo's ritziest neighborhood, soaked to the skin, toting backpacks and a baby, much to the horror of the doormen in their pristine suits and gloved hands. To their credit, they still managed the slightest of bows in our general direction as they swung open the heavy gilt and glass doors. That's the great thing about a Japanese bow. If you bend your neck at just the right angle to acknowledge even the feeblest respect, it saves you from having to make eye contact. They were well trained in the art of do not engage.

The reception staff checked us in with the utmost politeness, only their flaring nostrils betraying their disdain for the two grubby *gaijin*[1] creating puddles in front of their clean white counter. If it hadn't been for our pre-arranged booking, I think they would have ever so politely turned us away. The old no room at the inn trick. But alas... we were in.

Our room was on the tenth floor. I remember that distinctly for the oddest of reasons. An earthquake. As seasoned backpackers, we had rarely found ourselves in the midst of such luxury for a place to sleep. The ¥15,000 price tag, about $150 at the time, ensured that it would be for just one night, so prudently we took advantage of the handheld hot shower and deep Japanese tub to soak away the woes of the previous 12 hours. That took some time.

Our son, never one to sleep at the normal hours for his age, set about exploring the technologically enhanced accommodation, starting with the mini bar. Settling himself in front of the open fridge door, he liberated two cans of soft drink in quick succession simply by pressing on each one in turn, marveling at the way they fell at his feet and grinning from ear to ear. As I recklessly tried to reinsert them into their pigeonholes, another two swiftly popped out, sending my son into peals of laughter. What an excellent and expensive game. The blurb in the information folder informed me that drinks from the mini bar were automatically billed to the room via a sophisticated electronic link to the shelves in the fridge. Excellent news. We were already up for four unwanted cans of Coke and something called *Calpis*. Later we learned it was a fermented, fizzy milk drink, so it came to be known as cow-piss, though it actually tasted quite good.

A couple of hours later, after a good scrub and a long soak in water hot enough to boil eggs, I started to relax. I lay on the double bed in my hotel kimono admiring the neon view over this new city. The entire day had taken its weary toll. My eyelids were heavy and my limbs weak from all the walking, talking, carrying of packs and babies. The emotional scars were something else. The unwelcome words of the hotel manager I had spoken to on the phone earlier that evening were still ringing in my numb ears. *You will spend a lot of money if you don't have a plan.* It seemed he might be right after all.

It was well after 3 a.m., when without warning, the bed began to vibrate, a gentle, easy, side to side motion reminiscent of the old massage beds frequently found in cheap motels in the 70s. Alarmed at the thought of more yen being automatically added to our account, and assuming my son had somehow triggered a switch, I began frantically searching for a way to shut it down. But I couldn't find one.

As I looked at James in desperation, I noticed that the bed wasn't the only thing moving. The chandelier was also swaying from side to side. It was then that I realized we were experiencing our very first earthquake. Then, as quickly as it had begun, it stopped, and the room returned to an eerie quiet. Welcome to Japan, sitting squarely on the edge of the Pacific Ring of Fire.

Over the next few years we would become well-acquainted with the ups and downs of Japan's volcanic geography and learn that more is actually better when it comes to earthquakes. Upheavals every few days — pleasantly inconvenient. A couple of weeks with no movements — prepare for imminent disaster.

I lay back on the bed and my eyelids closed of their own accord, but my mind continued to replay the events of the day just gone, the conversations on an endless, torturous loop. Sleep still eluded me.

James sat zombie-like at the small work desk in the corner of the room, poring over the guidebooks and information pamphlets we had picked up at the airport reservation desk, looking for a cheaper option for our second night. He didn't find one, well, not one that was going to prolong our stay in Japan anyway. But he did find *Kimi Ryokan*.[2]

This pleasant, traditional Japanese inn located in a slightly less-expensive, leafy suburb near Roppongi came to our rescue. With a price tag about one-third that of the Ginza hotel, it became a base from which to make another thousand phone calls to what were affectionately termed *gaijin* houses, places where poor, broke backpackers like ourselves congregated in the hope of saving money by sharing the rent and utilities.

Then we found one, a former dormitory-style apartment house originally built by a local company to house their employees. It was located in the next prefecture, just across the Edo River, a half-hour train ride to the east of central Tokyo. Together with about 20 other international expatriates who already inhabited its rustic carcass, it would become our home for the next six months.

4
THE TALKING BUS

We were more than excited to finally find somewhere to call home, a more permanent and far less-expensive roof over our heads. And unlike the recipients of all those calls I'd made from the airport, these people actually seemed to be looking forward to the arrival of a baby. Before even meeting them, they restored my faith in humanity. But getting to our new abode in the Japanese 'burbs three days after our arrival in Tokyo proved to be another ride on the Japanese theme park roller coaster, aptly named The Talking Bus.

The manager of the *gaijin* house, Hans, had given James detailed instructions on how to get there.

"Catch the rapid train (that's the blue and white one) from Tokyo Station to Ichikawa. It takes about 20 minutes. When you get off the train, look for the *Daiei*[1] and make sure you exit on that side of the line. You'll see a bus loop where all the buses come and go. Head towards *Yamazaki*[2] and find the stand that says Matsudo. It's number 11. Get on that bus. After it leaves the bus stand, count the stops. They announce every stop, even if the bus doesn't stop there. Get off at stop number

17. You will have just passed a Skylark.³ Find a public phone. They're bright green. Call me again when you get that far."

When James relayed the instructions to me, I admit I was a bit deflated. Just the thought of returning to Tokyo Station brought back all the nightmares of our first night. And finding the right platform while dragging all our worldly belongings behind us sounded like another Herculean task. I went into sarcastic bitch mode.

"You've got to be kidding me. Does this place not have an address? Like, one that we can find on a map. I know the public phones are bright green because of the hours I spent on one a couple of days ago. But what the hell is a rapid train, a *Daiei*, and a Skylark?" They seemed like logical questions, but James had nothing more he could offer to placate me. After all, he'd never been there before either.

Negotiating Tokyo Station the second time around was actually a little less daunting. With the benefit of prior experience, we managed to find the correct platform and the said blue and white rapid train without major incident. And Ichikawa turned out to be exactly 19 minutes' journey on the JR Sobu line.

However, the manager had neglected to tell us several important things, things you just know if you have been in Japan longer than a few days. But we... we had no idea.

What was a *Daiei* when it was at home? Or a *Yamazaki* for that matter. We missed them completely. And there must have been at least a hundred buses coming and going in the loop. We could only guess at the destinations of the buses; apart from the number, everything was written in *kanji*,⁴ unreadable Chinese characters, and we had no idea what the ones that said Matsudo even looked like. And though they probably did announce each stop, they did so in Japanese, of course. Sometimes the announcements went on so long they ran into each other. If no one was getting off at that particular stop, the next announcement began straight away. It was impossible to count them. The bus just kept on talking.

So, there we were on this bus that wouldn't shut up. We had no idea where we were or where we were going, except maybe Matsudo, and no idea when to get off the bus. We had no landmarks to look out for other than a Skylark, whatever that looked like; last time I checked, it was some kind of bird. And which side of the road was it on, anyway? It was harrowing. A linguistic and transport stress far worse than any Indian bus or Chinese train could offer. I imagined us riding the infernal buses back and forth between Matsudo and Ichikawa forever, searching in vain for the illusory Skylark, doomed to this inscrutable nightmare for eternity.

While I silently wallowed in despair, James suddenly stood up, grabbed the backpacks and pulled on the cord running along the roof above our heads. "I think we better get off here."

"Why? Did you see a Skylark?" I looked out the window in earnest, hoping against hope to see that a giant statue of a bird had magically appeared.

"No. But it must be close. We'll just find a phone and call for further instructions." If only we'd known how that sentiment, the simple desire for further instructions, would define our lives for the next few years.

I followed James off the bus at the next stop, number whatever, and fell onto the sidewalk, having buckled under the weight of the bags and the baby while navigating the steep steps at the rear door of the bus. It took a few seconds to gather myself off the ground, but after I determined that the gash on my arm was only skin deep, and that the baby had survived the fall unscathed, my first question was, "Well, which direction should we walk now, do you think?" It was more of a rhetorical question, but one that was loaded with blame. What I was really saying was, "It was your decision to get off the bus here in the middle of bloody nowhere, so what's your next smart-ass move?" Sarcastic bitch can be quite cruel when she's upset, confused, stressed, and thoroughly pissed. It's not a common occurrence, but when travel plans go south, she can appear out of the blue, ready to cut down all and sundry with a fierce tongue. This was one of those times. It felt like the universe was out to get me, and I was furious at the injustice of it all. In situations such as this, I wanted someone to blame. Poor James!

James suggested we just walk till we came to a phone, which fortunately seemed to be dotted along the road with monotonous, fluro-green frequency. There was one just up ahead. When we reached it, he called the house again. He must have sounded distressed, exhausted, and desperate all rolled into one because Hans decided to come find us. He said he would be at the corner in ten minutes. We just weren't sure which corner that would be, and whether we would be anywhere within sight when he got there.

Right on cue, about ten minutes later, he did pop up and he was about 100 yards down the road, back the way we had come. He greeted us warmly, lifted one of the packs onto his back, and guided us down the hill through a maze of narrow lanes and alleyways to the house, which we would never have found on our own. Based on our experiences so far, I was beginning to think we would probably be lost for our entire stay in Japan.

5

GAIJIN HOUSE

*E*ven from right out front, it was hard to see the two-story house. A narrow gravel path lined with bicycles of all shapes and sizes led through the overgrown garden to the front entrance. Soon I would come to realize that this maze of untamed weeds and bamboo stands was a blessing in disguise. It protected the residents from being the focal point of a very suburban enclave and an ongoing source of entertainment for our Japanese neighbors.

"Take off your shoes here." Hans removed his own shoes with the practiced art of a veteran. He placed them neatly onto a shelf in a narrow cupboard before stepping up into a pair of plastic slippers that appeared to be waiting for him. They were even facing the right way to just step straight into. For me, the same exercise involved flopping down heavily on the step, baby still on my back, straining to reach forward and fumble awkwardly with my shoelaces. It was far from graceful, but slightly more composed than my dismount from the talking bus. I made a mental note-to-self to never ever wear lace up shoes for the rest of my time in Japan.

"What happened to your arm?" Hans had noticed the trickle of blood winding around my elbow.

"The freaking talking bus happened," I muttered under my breath. Then loudly enough for him to actually hear, I answered, "Oh nothing. It's just a flesh wound." Self-effacement would actually turn out to be a good quality to have in Japan.

"We have a first aid kit in the tool room. You can clean it up later. Come, everyone is waiting for you." We stepped up into the house and followed him through a narrow door and hallway that opened into the dining room and kitchen.

When the good people of the house heard a baby was going to take up residence, they had all waited in for us to arrive, a stark contrast to that ill-fated afternoon of phone calls from the airport arrivals hall that now seemed to belong to the dim past. Mani played the *gaijin* game extremely well, beaming widely when we entered the room and found it full of friendly, smiling strangers. He was an instant hit. It was to be the first of many such encounters in store for us and him in Japan, accosted by hordes of strangers all yelling *kawaii*[1] and wanting to touch his golden hair. Luckily, he wasn't perturbed by this behavior, taking it in his stride and enjoying the attention. I did wonder about the consequences of such open and overwhelming adoration and whether he would come to expect this reaction to his presence everywhere in the world. It could have become quite a problem.

The residents were a mixed bunch: German, Dutch, Canadian, Israeli, American, and several other Aussies. Now leased by a Japanese businessman for the express purpose of providing a home away from home for a melting pot of nations, the house had once been home to a gaggle of *salarymen,* the Japanese term for husbands and fathers who spent their days working for the man. There were 18 rooms on two levels, and about 20 residents in total.

Because the house was always on the brink of overflowing and usually had a long waiting list, Hans had pulled a few strings with the Japanese leaseholder to move us into the the one recently vacated room at the rear of the lower floor. To circumvent the waiting list, residents would often share with friends until such time as a room became available. Consequently, there was often a surplus of one particular nationality, which eventually became an issue. So, at a monthly house meeting, the residents voted to limit the number of people of each nationality allowed in the house at any one time. Yes, it really was that big an issue.

The main problem was the language barrier. If there were a preponderance of one nationality preparing a meal in the kitchen, or eating in the adjacent dining room, or watching TV together, their native tongue was the language of the moment. If that happened to be a language that several people spoke, it was a minor issue. But when it was something more obscure like Flemish, Swahili, or even Korean, interlopers were instantly, if accidentally, ostracized. It caused some ill-will from time to time.

Some of the residents were colorful, to say the very least. Most of the young women worked at the hostess bars in central Tokyo. It was mundane work that paid quite well, and simply involved sitting around tables with local businessmen all evening, lighting their cigarettes, making sure their glasses were always full, and providing idle chit chat in English. Some of the more upmarket establishments required the girls to engage in *dohan*,[2] a one-on-one dinner date, on a weekly or fortnightly basis. The girls didn't like it, but they put up with it to keep their jobs. And things rarely became awkward, if you know what I mean.

The guys, on the other hand, mostly worked either as English teachers or in the parades at Tokyo Disneyland. One house member had the prestigious role of Prince Charming because, evidently, Prince Charming could never be Japanese. Likewise, the girls who played Cinderella, Snow White, and Red Riding Hood were also foreigners.

After the girls had all departed for their evening shifts at the bars, I was often left alone with the washing up. It had been pointed out to me on several occasions that it wasn't my job to clean up after anyone, but in reality, if I wanted to cook my own dinner, I had to. It did start to wear thin after a while, but I tried to see it as a trade-off for everyone being so patient with the energetic antics of my one-year-old son. It was a small price to pay.

I always felt quite safe in Japan, whether walking around alone, riding my bike at night, or at home by myself. One evening not long after we arrived, I went to check out a commotion at the front door. Standing before me in the semi-darkness, removing a pair of cute pumps was a giant of a figure with straight, jet black hair that appeared to be awkwardly tied to her head with an equally giant Minnie Mouse bow. Though she was mostly silhouetted against the porch light, I could tell she was wearing a skirt that reached well above her knees and a short jacket. Something about the huge bow on her head led me to assume she must also work at Disneyland and had decided to come home in costume, though the reasoning behind such a move escaped me.

I didn't have much time to ponder the whys and wherefores of that before she noticed me watching her perform the shoe-removal ritual in the entrance. When she opened her mouth to greet me, her voice was dark and timbered and blew me back just a noticeable amount. She identified herself as Tina. Quickly, I regained composure, and introduced myself and my son.

I got to know Tina quite well over the next few months, as we were frequently the only ones home in the early evening. She was a long-term resident of the house, working as an English teacher and a Polish translator in equal measures. Everyone, including the Japanese, accepted her as just another crazy member of the unique *gaijin* family of which we were all a part.

Being a house full of *bakka gaijin*,[3] we were objects of intense interest for the local residents. One young man in particular couldn't help himself and felt the urge to sneak around peering in our windows on a nightly basis. Though he appeared to be harmless, he was still disturbing. And possibly also a little disturbed. Everyone knew about him; we dubbed him The Stalker. He used to wait till after dark then creep around in the bushes surrounding the house. It was very hard to go unnoticed in the thick, crackly undergrowth. We always knew he was there because of the sound of snapping twigs.

We were still living in the downstairs room when we first encountered The Stalker. It was late; we had just turned in for the night and were lying in the dark. Some of the girls were still awake and chatting quietly in the TV room upstairs. In the warm night stillness, their voices carried out the windows and down over the gardens. Everyone was unwinding after the hot summer day.

A loud rustling outside our window drew everyone's attention, and voices from the upstairs windows began yelling abuse. Even in English, the stalker could be in no doubt about the meaning of the words hurled his way. But then I had a bright idea.

Oh so quietly, I felt around in the dark for my camera. In the four-and-a-half-mat room, most of our possessions were within easy reach. I thought if I could snap a picture of him, it might just scare him off for good. Knowing that we had him on film could be a big deterrent. I found the tiny Canon with built in flash and switched it on. It whirred into action as the flash warmed up. When it was ready, I crawled over to the open window and aimed into the darkness in the direction of the last sound of rustling bushes. Snap! The whole outdoor area lit up like daylight and a startled figure took off through the bushes as if he had been shot, rustling leaves and snapping branches as he rocketed away. Clapping and cheering exploded from the rooms above me. Stalker exposed and frightened to death.

We didn't see him around the house again for the rest of our time there. But we also didn't get to learn his identity from the resulting photograph. Luckily for him, the fly screen on the window had diffused all the light from the flash and reflected it back into the lens, leaving an obscure image with a bright white center. Nevertheless, it achieved the desired outcome — stalker-free evenings for the rest of the summer.

Over the next few months, our house mates taught us some of the ins and outs of Japanese life: how to set up a futon, what to do with the slippers provided inside the house, where to shop and when, how to save money on basic food items, where to get our own bicycles for free, how to get back into Tokyo city, how to navigate the subway system, where to go and what to see, what to do in an earthquake, and most importantly, how to get a job. There were lots of tricks and lots of rules, Japanese rules. And we had lots to learn.

Life with a young baby in a foreign country required lots of adjusting. We didn't have a car and baby seats, or even a pram or stroller. In fact, I had none of the paraphernalia that usually accompanies the arrival of a new baby. Not long after we arrived, one of my new housemates quizzed me about that lack of implements and accessories. We were all attending a spontaneous get-together down on the banks of the Edo River late one afternoon, along with several long-term expats and previous house residents. Phil had lived in the *gaijin* house several years before, but early on in his stay he had fallen in love with Naoko, whom he met through one of his students. They had since married and were expecting their first child.

"Do you mind if I ask you something?" Phil approached me as I stood watching Mani play.

"Not at all," I replied.

"My wife is Japanese. She's about six-months pregnant right now and our house is literally filling up with all the things we 'need' to accommodate a new baby." I smiled. I knew where this was going. "Yet here you are, just arrived in a country where you know no one, can't speak the language, and you brought with you just two backpacks and a baby carrier. How on earth does that work?"

"I'll let you in on a little secret." I smiled again. "You don't need any of it. You really don't. A few baby clothes, some diapers, and a breast full of milk. That's it."

"Unbelievable. Maybe you could tell my wife that." He walked away, shaking his head.

But it was true.

∼

6

JOURNAL

April 17

My first chance to write since we arrived. We've only been here a week, so everything is new and exciting, everything is a learning experience. Today is the first nice spring day we have seen; it has been raining almost every day since we arrived. On top of this, our first days in Tokyo were an absolute nightmare. Because of the influx of tourists and travelers alike at this time of year (think cherry blossoms), Tokyo is jam-packed. After six hours on the telephone at Narita International Airport (inconveniently located about 40 miles from Tokyo), we had no choice but to take a hotel room for $150 plus 10% service charge and pay $15 a head on the airport limousine bus to get there. Several irritated voices on the other end of the phone had taken obvious pleasure in pointing out the expense of Tokyo. We're going to need our wits about us at all times.

Somehow, we have found a permanent home in a gaijin house despite the long waiting list to get in. It's a comfortable, Japanese-style house, leased by a Japanese man and operated on a share basis by the people who stay here. Everyone here is in Japan for economic reasons and for quite long periods, so they treat the house as a home, not just a hotel or guest house.

There are 18 tatami-style rooms accommodating about 20 people; the floors are made of straw matting (tatami) and each night we unroll our futon for sleeping. There are a few Israelis, some Canadians, another Aussie, a German couple, a Dutch couple, us, and someone nobody is quite sure about who lives in the room next to ours.

The house is well-equipped with great hot showers, a washing machine, darkroom, work room, kitchen, sewing machine, radiators, fans. The whole place has been fitted out from the gomi, the Japanese term for trash. The Japanese continually update their consumer goods, and the old ones, maybe just 12 months old, are put out on the local rubbish pile once a month. Enter the resourceful gaijin. The TV and stereo in the common room, still going strong after two years, were both rescued from a local pile. Several of the guys in the house have been known to stand beside the piles trying on perfectly good suits, tossed out in their dry-cleaning plastic. In fact, today we're going to look for bicycles. They throw them out when they have a flat tire; not even a puncture, just a flat. This system is quite beneficial for us, as absolutely everything is expensive.

Yesterday we revisited central Tokyo. We're only 20 minutes from the CBD, but it's much quieter and more aesthetic out here. James had an interview in town for a teaching job, but it involves quite a bit of traveling, so he is looking for something else that doesn't. A lot of time is wasted flying around Tokyo on the subway, and though the employers usually pay the fares, they don't pay for travel time. The going rate with 'qualifications' is ¥4,000 per hour ($40) but finding jobs with enough hours per week is tough. There are literally thousands of language schools and lots of competition for the jobs on offer.

Everyone seems to love the idea of a baby living here. The day we arrived, Mani had a welcoming committee who had waited in to greet him. With all the different languages spoken here, we don't know whether his first words will be in Hebrew, English, German, or Japanese. It's hard to stop people from feeding him sweets and biscuits; they all think he is very kawaii.[1]

We have had two earth tremors since we arrived, one on our first night in Tokyo and one on our first night here. It's quite a nice sensation, a bit like those vibrating beds they used to have in some motels, only the movement is more noticeable. Sideways is no problem; up-and-down movement means it's a bigger one. They happen sometimes two or three times a week then maybe nothing for a month. Everyone likes to be awake when they happen, as you don't notice them if you're asleep. I guess it's a novelty we'll get used to and not look forward to.

Moving to Japan has been an overwhelming experience on many levels. Every moment has brought new challenges, challenges that have made me question whether this may not have been a good idea. At the very least, we should have made better plans, perhaps even some bookings. The footloose and fancy-free approach that worked so well on the back roads of India and Southeast Asia is not effective here. It just ends up being expensive.

Until we managed to find this room in the gaijin house, I felt defeated by the consequences of our decisions, out of my league, and definitely way past my comfort zone. Only since we've moved into the expat community of the house, our little shared island in the unknown outside, have things begun to look up and our long-term prospects started to improve. Acceptance of our little family has been a big part of that, especially after the initial, flat out rejection and dismissal we faced at Narita Airport.

While I'm still wary of the cost of living here, I'm beginning to feel more confident that we can make a go of this experience and immerse ourselves in this unique culture. Time will tell.

∽

7
HOUSE RULES

*L*iving in a Japanese-style house, especially one shared by so many different nationalities, necessitated lots of rules — rules about what to wear on your feet and when, how to make your futon bed, what to do with it during the day, rules about keeping your food in the kitchen, how to navigate the bathroom and toilet, and which language to speak in the common areas, as mentioned in Chapter 4.

Rule #1 — Shoes

I had always thought that the Japanese didn't wear shoes inside. That's a myth. Living in a Japanese-style house is a bit of a soft shoe shuffle. The only place where shoes are definitely not allowed is on the *tatami*;[1] when you see them for the first time, you understand why. They consist of a thin, finely woven layer of soft rush straw, edged in silk brocade, sitting atop a wooden frame traditionally packed with rice straw. Floors are purposely recessed to accommodate them, as they are about 4-5 inches thick. Placing them in a room is a bit like doing a jigsaw puzzle. Every piece has its place. And they only fit together one way.

Only bare feet, socks, or stockings are permitted on *tatami*, since wearing shoes on such a delicate surface breaks the tiny straw fibers and destroys the mat. Furniture can have a similar effect. And *tatami* are not cheap. Authentic, hand-made varieties can cost over ¥150,000 each (about $1,500).

So, definitely no shoes or slippers on *tatami* mats.

However, indoor slippers are allowed everywhere else. Except the bathroom. Typically, slippers are lined up in the *genkan*,[2] ready to step straight into as you step up into the house proper, just as Hans had done so deftly the night we arrived. And you can wear these all around the house. But on entering the bathroom or toilet, these must also be removed, and another pair of plastic slippers donned while using the facilities. But don't forget to remove the plastic slippers on the way out. Walking around the house in bathroom slippers is particularly frowned upon, not to mention unsanitary.

So, even in your own home, you're constantly stepping in and out of shoes and slippers. It's no wonder that many young Japanese wander around outside with their shoelaces mostly undone, or at least very loosely tied. It's just easier to get in and out of them.

Walking around outside without shoes is almost as big a crime as wearing shoes on *tatami*, and likely to call your sanity into question. An Aussie friend of mine tried it once, and only once, because everyone she passed on her way to the park stopped and asked her if she was okay, eyeing her bare feet skeptically while voicing their concern for her mental health.

Rule #2 — Bathroom Etiquette

Following on from the rules about shoes, Japanese bathroom protocol also took a bit of getting used to, but the rules were quite simple once explained. The tub was deep and the water hot, heated by an outdoor gas heater after being filled with cold water. It took about an hour to heat up and then it was covered with boards or a roll-back plastic lid to keep it hot. A small wooden stool was provided for seated comfort while you used the handheld shower to wash yourself prior to climbing into the tub and having a good old soak. Everyone used the same water, so you had to be thoroughly and spotlessly scrubbed and every trace of soap removed before getting into the tub.

It was impossible to spend too long in there though. Apart from coming out looking like a cooked lobster, there were at least ten other people waiting on the luxury of a hot soak. So, you couldn't get too relaxed, which kind of defeated the purpose.

Rule #3 — Kitchen Etiquette

With so many people sharing the house, the kitchen and dining areas were highly organized, starting with the fridges. There were four of these in various shapes and sizes, which may sound extravagant, but all of them had been rescued from the monthly rubbish collections at one time or another. Everyone had at least one shelf on which to keep their personal food items. And woe betide anyone caught consuming food from a shelf other than their own. Universally used condiments, such as salt, pepper, sugar, and soy sauce were purchased by the manager for communal enjoyment.

It was everyone's responsibility to clean up after themselves, but at peak times, when everyone was in a massive rush to catch the train to work, that rule was almost invariably ignored.

Rule #4 — How to Live in a Tiny Room

An interesting quirk of Japanese architecture is that room sizes are measured in mats — *tatami* mats —measuring approximately three feet by six feet. This has the effect of standardizing everything from rugs and carpets to furniture. Typical room sizes are four-and-a-half, six, eight, and the unbelievably huge twelve-mat rooms. Almost no one has a twelve-mat room because that would mean owning the equivalent of the Taj Mahal. Even the communal TV room at the house was only an eight-mat room. Most of the rooms, our living quarters, were just four-and-a-half mats each. There was a bathroom on each level, a dark room for the photography geeks (go figure), a tool room, a dining room, and a shared kitchen.

Even our compact room had a massive floor-to-ceiling cupboard with sliding paper doors and was divided into three horizontal sections by two interior shelves. The space underneath the first shelf, roughly half the size of the cupboard, was supposed to store the bedding during the day, otherwise there would be no room to actually live in. Because we had a crawling baby with a very active daily agenda, we turned the bottom half of the cupboard into Mani's private playroom filled with all his toys and decorated the walls with random art works and colorful, printed cloth panels. The top shelf held our backpacks and any associated paraphernalia we didn't need that often in the course of everyday life. This was just as well, since I couldn't reach it without standing on a chair, an action which would have left deep indents in the flooring. The middle section of the cupboard was for everything else, which for us meant only our clothes. The entire contents of the one backpack we had arrived in the country with didn't take up much room, so we had quite a bit of space to play with.

Over time, and after a few good *gomi*[3] raids, we accumulated enough furniture to fill the rest of the room. One of our most prized rescued possessions was a *kotatsu*, a low coffee table with a heater attached to the underside of the frame. The tabletop could be removed, and a cozy blanket placed underneath it. At least four people could then sit around it, legs and feet under the blanket, being warmed by the heater. Everyone had one that they'd rescued from the *gomi* at one time or another. They were the perfect solution to a cool winter evening at home. Add in a couple of *tatami* chairs (padded seats with backs and arms but no legs) and the living was easy. A practical Japanese solution to life on the floor of a house made of paper and wood.

Rule #5 — Bowing

Long before we ever visited Japan, we met a young Japanese man on a working holiday in Sydney. When we quizzed him about customs in his home country, he told us that no one bowed any more. After just a few days in Tokyo, I was convinced he must have come from another planet, because not only was bowing still in vogue, it was universal. Everybody bowed, many times a day, every time they said thank you, or goodbye, or hello, or anything really. It was only the length and depth of the bow that varied. And that depended on the social hierarchy of the interaction.

Some bows were mere nods of the head, an acknowledgement of interference in another's space, or a minor inconvenience. Sometimes the nod was accompanied by a hand gesture and a verbal apology (*sumimasen*).[4] Placing your palm perpendicular to your forehead and in front of your bowed head around nose level indicated you were going to push your way through a crowd. Shop staff lined the entrance to stores and bowed deeply as the first customers streamed in through the doors at opening time. Young people bowed to older people as a mark of respect, and older people bowed to each other for the same reason. Sometimes it appeared to be a battle of wills to see who would relinquish their bow first.

Bowing was most certainly alive and well in Japan and learning the rules of engagement was a minefield that often left me feeling completely incompetent. Keep calm and carry on bowing.

Lots More Rules

There were many other social norms unique to Japanese society. Though we would never presume to understand all of them, sometimes it was hard to know which ones we should strive to uphold, and our choices often landed us in situations that were both frustrating and ridiculously complicated.

Take opening a bank account for example. As you would expect, no one at the local bank branch spoke English. There was a little uniformed man stationed by the door whose job it was to offer assistance and help negotiate the teller queues and ATMs. He was always polite and congenial, but he couldn't help that much unless you spoke Japanese. Not that we were complaining about that. I can't imagine any bank teller in my own country being conversant with financial terms in a foreign language, let alone Japanese. So, fair's fair.

But a peculiarity of the Japanese banking system demanded that to open an account the customer should present in person at the bank with their official *hanko*.[5] These small cylinders, usually made of wood or polished marble (or even ivory in some decadent cases), were engraved on one end with the Japanese characters of the person's surname and stamped onto documents in red ink in lieu of a signature. Obviously, these were highly valuable and needed to be securely protected at all costs. Losing one was akin to losing your signature, and effectively, your identity. All kinds of fraudulent activities could be perpetrated in your name if your *hanko* fell into the wrong hands. You could even end up divorced without knowing it.

Mass-produced and custom-made *hanko* could easily be purchased from shops that specialized in the trade. Common Japanese surnames were easy to find. So, it seemed an easy solution to just pick up one of those in any name whatsoever and use it to open a bank account. Several residents of the *gaijin* house had successfully acquired a bank account this way. But it proved problematic if the said *hanko* was lost. Purchasing another one, exactly the same as the one that was lost was not an option. It seemed that not all *hanko* were created equal. And Japanese tellers were highly skilled at identifying one from another, even though to our untrained eyes they appeared to be identical.

We elected to have one custom made using characters of our own choosing. The locals always pronounced our surname *ha-ke-to*, so I spent many hours poring over my *kanji* dictionary searching for just the right combination of characters to replicate those sounds and still have a significant meaning. I settled on three characters that could be pronounced appropriately, and roughly translated to 'the way that reflects the spirit'. Nice, I thought. But it earned me only blank looks from the locals. No one got it, largely because there was no such word in Japanese. What I had failed to understand was that you can't just stick characters together to come up with a meaning you prefer. There were rules, and I had ignored them all in my search for an obscure, spiritual significance.

When the friendly doorman at the local branch of the Chiba Bank finally understood what we had come to the bank to do, he was a little nervous. But when he saw our *hanko*, his face lit up. We had the requisite piece of the puzzle that was the key to the Japanese banking system. The rest was mere paperwork. We had spared him the embarrassment of having to turn us away. We were in.

We found ourselves in situations like this over and over again during our time in Japan, situations where towing the line and following the rules was the best and only response. It often went against the grain, and sometimes the rules seemed ridiculous to our Western minds, but we discovered that if you simply embraced the way Japanese society worked, the wheels turned, and things got done. There was no inscrutable, magic bullet after all.

8

RAIDERS OF THE LOST GOMI

*O*ur housemates wasted no time in introducing us to several concepts unique to Japan. The best and most fortuitous of these for new arrivals struggling to make sense of the exchange rate without breaking down in tears was *gomi* — garbage, rubbish, and trash in any other language. Just the thought of uncovering recycled riches sent normally quiet, unobtrusive introverts into raptures over the mountains of unburied treasure that appeared on the sidewalks of the city roughly once a month. It was one of the best things about living in Japan in the 1980s, not least of which was because it saved us so much money.

Gomi was much more than just rubbish. It was more like an all-encompassing term for anything you didn't want or no longer needed. It could be scraps from your kitchen, such as veggie peelings and empty containers, any of the millions of pieces of plastic and paper packaging accumulated while shopping (and that really was *gomi*) or household items, such as furniture, ornaments, electrical appliances, clothing, and even bicycles. It was like having unlimited access to a store full of free stuff. And every self-respecting, long-term resident *gaijin* loved it and lived for the monthly *gomi* raids, as they had become known.

The Japanese had devised a very efficient system for getting rid of *gomi* and provided every household with a poster that displayed the rules and regulations pictorially. That was a bonus, since our understanding of the written language was non-existent in the early days. Kitchen rubbish, considered to be burnable, was to be disposed of in large paper bags tied up with string, and placed at the nearest *gomi* station on the appropriate days of the week, typically three times a week. Plastic rubbish, which included anything that couldn't be burned, was collected only twice a week. This seemed a little unusual and inconvenient, since the amount of plastic rubbish we accumulated while shopping far outweighed the amount of burnable rubbish we discarded in the kitchen. Yet it wasn't collected as often. Big *gomi* collections only took place once a month, and that was the day we all looked forward to. We cruised the streets checking out the offerings by light of day, then went out in groups under cover of darkness to pick over the discards of our Japanese neighbors.

Now, I know you might be thinking, "Gross! Going through other people's trash and actually taking it home with you." But let me assure you, this was not your usual trash. The main reason for the size and quality of the piles was directly attributable to the Japanese concept of shame. It was not considered kosher to offer another person your cast-offs, since this would imply that you thought badly of that person or thought they might be unable to afford their own things. And the condition of the goods was immaterial. They could be brand new, but if you no longer wanted or needed them, it would be rude to offer them to someone else. Perhaps for this reason, it was hard to locate second-hand stores in Tokyo, though there was the odd one around. But the clientele always seemed to be noticeably awkward about being seen there. So, this, coupled with the local penchant for the latest model everything no doubt added to the high-quality of the pickings.

Most of the furniture and appliances in the *gaijin* house had come from the *gomi*. The fridges, as mentioned before, the toasters, the small gas burners and griller ovens, the TV and stereo, the washing machines, the lounges, the futons, the dark room equipment. It was pickers' heaven. Some of the more extreme piles extended over half a block, making it almost impossible to get a car down the narrow streets. Every month, every resident could be seen returning to the house at odd hours of the night with new treasures to decorate their tiny rooms.

Some of the rescued items were somewhat harder to overlook, notably the two huge paper lanterns hanging from the ceiling of the TV room. They were over three feet in length and each had the same three exquisitely painted Japanese characters down one side. Everyone who entered the room for the first time was in awe of their beauty. Everyone except the Japanese, that is. They knew exactly what they were. Though it was initially unknown to the residents of the house who rescued them from the *gomi*, the lanterns were actually decorations from a funeral. And the three lovely *kanji* painted on them? They spelt out the name of the recently deceased.

Many of us used the TV room to teach and entertain our English language students. It was big and roomy and comfortable and, of course, it housed those beautiful hanging lanterns. But oh, if I had a dollar for every time a Japanese student entered that room and almost fainted in shock. But being the reprobates we were, with our twisted senses of humor, we all thought it was kind of amusing, if somewhat irreverent. We meant no offense.

So, the moral of the story was be careful what you find lurking on sidewalks late at night amid piles of trash. Some of it might actually be trash.

9

GETTING HIRED

$\mathcal{O}$nce we had fully settled into the *gaijin* house and worked out the lay of the land as best we could, the next task was to find a job. The best source of information, apart from those already in employment in the house, was the classified section of *The Japan Times*. It was a hot property in the house, especially on Mondays when it sported a large classified section in the back pages, advertising lots of English language teaching positions.

A lot of the jobs were posted by English conversation schools and *juku*, commonly known as cram schools. They operated outside of school hours, and beleaguered Japanese students from elementary school all the way up to high school age, were routinely enrolled by their parents for after school tutorial classes. I was told that getting into the right university, meaning either the University of Tokyo or Waseda University, was more important than the actual course of study. In fact, some schools acted as elevator schools for these particular tertiary institutions. If you scored a place in one of the preferred primary or secondary institutions, you were practically guaranteed a place in the hallowed halls of the associated university. Working in a *juku*, however, wasn't all it was cracked up to be. Long hours, late nights, and easily distracted students were par for the course. It was eminently more lucrative to land a job in an English conversation school.

Getting an interview was only half the battle. Locating the school was the tricky part. This was solely due to the fact that the Japanese address system was not arranged numerically. As I understood it, addresses were assigned either chronologically or in a clockwise direction. With the latter system, numbers were sometimes skipped to allow for further construction. Hence, the first building erected in the suburb often had the lowest lot number, and additional or subsequent constructions on the same lot were simply given the same lot number followed by a hyphen and another number. For example, Shinjuku 210-1 was not necessarily next door to Shinjuku 210-2, although it probably was in the same general area. And depending on the size of the lot, there could be up to ten or twenty hyphenated addresses for the same lot number. To the uninitiated, it was extremely confusing.

So, instructions on how to get to a particular address went something like this: Take the Yamanote line (the green train) to Shinjuku station and exit on the side of the station where you see the Isetan department store. Shinjuku station is one of the largest in the world and millions of passengers pass through it every day. Finding an exit, any exit, is a feat of monumental proportions on its own. There are around 200 of them. Combine this with the fact that you don't really know which way is up or down when you alight onto one of the 20 platforms and you can understand the potential to be lost inside the station for days. Taking the Yamanote line does have its advantages though, since it is one of the few that circle central Tokyo above ground. That makes it a bit easier to spot the department store referenced in the instructions.

The instructions continue: After exiting, walk to the left until you come to a 7-Eleven store on a corner. Cross the road diagonally at the scramble[1] (what the hell is a scramble?) and keep walking to the left. When you come to the Mr. Donut cafe, you'll see a doorway with a set of stairs leading to the first floor. Come upstairs to the school reception area.

Getting Hired

James went to one of his first conversation school interviews alone. About the time he should have been seated across a table from the head teacher and chief administrator, I got a phone call.

"Are you done already? How did it go?" I asked.

"It didn't. I can't find the damn place." I could hear the frustration in his voice.

"Well, have you called to get better instructions?" Obvious question perhaps.

"I've called three bloody times. I still can't find it. I give up. I'm coming home."

He did manage to find that particular school at a later date, but it took three trips into Tokyo, only to find the job was wholly unsuitable. It was a pattern that would play out several times over the first month of our stay. As we watched our meagre funds rapidly dwindle, we began to fear that getting a job in the city was almost impossible. Several times we questioned the futility of it all, wondering whether the income-producing machine that was rumored to be Tokyo's English conversation obsession had dried up in the wake of over-saturation. It spoke to the desperation of the Japanese to learn English that even Hebrew-speaking Israelis with thick accents were able to find English-teaching positions. While James waited for the right job to come along, he made do with private lessons handed over by other residents of the *gaijin* house who, for one reason or another, couldn't keep their appointments. It was enough to survive on. Just.

Then one Monday morning, *The Japan Times* classified gods smiled our way, and printed an advertisement for teachers at the Berlitz Schools of Languages Japan (Inc.). Oh, happy day! James applied, found the interview location easily, and was hired on the spot. Our prospects, and our attitudes to life in the Land of the Rising Sun, dramatically and instantly improved. What a difference a job makes.

Berlitz was far and away one of the more prestigious language schools in the country and they had a fairly constant demand for teachers of English and, to a lesser extent, most other modern languages. They also offered a ten-day paid training course in the Berlitz Method, which demanded exclusive use of the target language in the classroom, and a lucrative monthly contract. They had schools all over the city as well as dotted around the rest of Japan, but the best part was that they were about to open a new school in Matsudo, just down the road.

James' initial contract was for thirty 40-minute lessons a week, scheduled between the hours of 1:45 and 9:10 p.m. They weren't all at the same school, so there was a bit of traveling involved, but that was also paid. Another bonus was that most of the lessons were one-on-one, less stressful than the privately arranged groups that often numbered up to 30 students all at different levels and abilities. Under such circumstances, teacher was a very loose term. Improv entertainer was probably a more appropriate job title.

The Berlitz contract came with other benefits, namely health insurance for the three of us and two weeks' paid vacation each year. It was a fantastic opportunity. Once the new school opened, James spent his afternoons teaching in Tokyo and his evenings at the new school in Matsudo, calling in at the house for dinner on his way through. It was a perfect arrangement.

I filled my days roaming around the 'burbs on my bicycle with Mani, finding new supermarkets and grocery stores, exquisite temples, and teeny playgrounds. I guess it was a lonely life, but I scarcely noticed. Many of my friends back home would have given their right arm for the luxury of staying home with their kids. And I delighted in my son despite his constant busy-ness. I could always retreat to the safety and comfort of the *gaijin* house and its residents when the need for adult interaction surfaced. It helped that James and I had become fairly insular over the course of our extended travels, having largely forgone the familiar bonds of family and friendship for an itinerant, international lifestyle. It was a trade-off that suited our needs at the time and served me well during our first year in Japan. I would pay for it in other ways, but I didn't know it at the time.

10

JOURNAL

May 23

Time gets away so quickly. Mani is turning into a little boy before my eyes and I guess he'll be grown up before we can blink. He knows no fear, which is a bad thing now that he has learnt to climb the stairs. We have to be constantly vigilant or he's up there in a flash, beaming victoriously from the middle levels. I fear that when he starts to walk, we'll have to start running. There are plenty of dangers in the house, things you would pay no mind unless you had an inquisitive toddler.

We've settled into the gaijin house quite cozily now. And we've moved rooms. An Israeli couple left last week and bequeathed us their old room. It looks out onto a leafy garden, which lets in lovely filtered sunlight in the afternoon. Much more aesthetic than the noisy motor repair shop on the other side of the house.

The floor is where it's at here, so we feel right at home. Shoes at the main door, house shoes inside, socks or bare feet on the tatami, and special shoes for the toilet, which is a non-flushing, squat variety that needs to be vacuumed out on a regular basis by the men in the shit truck. We can easily tell when they're in the neighborhood.

Our bicycles are getting lots of use, riding down to the station to do our shopping, around the streets looking for new and exciting gomi, and generally exploring the area. Apart from main thoroughfares, streets in Tokyo are just wide enough for one car, so it's nice to have the freedom to ride around and soak up the wa without having to worry too much about traffic. We must have looked a sight on our late-night escapade to adopt the abandoned bikes. James rode one bike while trying to steer another at the same time, and I rode shotgun on a makeshift seat far too low for the bike, looking for all the world like Evil Knievel in drag. Rain made it all the more unpleasant.

James is doing the training course with Berlitz this week, which means he's been going to Tokyo every day on peak hour trains. They're so crowded that everyone sleeps standing up. He says there's no chance of falling over because you can't move. When the train slows for a station, everyone collapses in a heap, having nothing but each other to hang onto. If you happen to be near the door when the train stops, you have no option but to get off so that people stuck in the middle of the carriage can also alight. The men employed to push people onto the trains actually spend more of their time pulling people off.

It's rumored that 12 million people pass through the barriers at Shinjuku station, the largest in Tokyo, every day. That's equivalent to the whole population of the city. Chinese buses were empty by comparison. It's hard to get a seat at any time of the day and the last train at midnight is just as bad as peak hour. In a city this size, it's hard to believe that the rail network shuts down at midnight.

We had a bonus from the gomi the other day. There amid a stack of stereos and TVs, boxes of crockery and ordinary household junk, lay a bag of clothes; inside were two suits, still with dry-cleaning tags, and four or five pairs of jeans. It was a real find. The suit jackets will come in handy for James when he's teaching, although the pants are a bit short for him.

I'm waiting to hear about some editing/rewriting work I applied for on a take-home basis. It's a slow process putting together piecemeal hours and having a baby doesn't help matters. I just have to keep trying, I guess.

The cost of living here is very high, in fact, one of the most expensive in the world, but the standards are just as high. As a group, the Japanese can be homogeneous, predictable, and ultra-conservative. Conformity is the key word. I haven't seen one scrap of graffiti in this city. I'm sure that must say something about the Japanese mind.

We were all discussing the Japanese mind in the dining room last night, from our purely Western perspectives, of course. They love to start sentences with 'We Japanese...' when they are explaining some weird and wonderful custom. It starts to grate after a while, as it implies 'We Foreigners' could never possibly understand. And maybe that's true.

Someone in the round table discussion commented that they thought the truth had very little relevance or value in Japanese society. Lies, glaringly obvious ones as well as little white ones, are tolerated for the sake of harmony – the communal wa. And because they are often more palatable than the truth. If you say what everyone wants to hear, everyone can be happy. It seems pretty false, and you may never know that your friend really detests you. It's just one opinion, and from an outsider at that.

It's hard to come to any conclusions about the country or the people at this stage because we are all on the outside. And that's what gaijin literally means — outside person. For this reason, I may never truly understand Japanese society and how it works but I have been given a gift of insight into a culture dramatically different from my own and I am determined to make the most of it. Coming to terms with my reactions and interactions will take more time.

11

A YEN FOR SAVINGS

*O*ur fellow housemates tended to stay in Japan for a long time, even if that hadn't been their original intention. It certainly wasn't ours during that first year. We were there to make some money and get back to the real business of life — traveling. At first it seemed as if that might not happen, but it did eventually pan out for us and our savings started to pile up. We were so focused on the big picture and so used to living on the smell of an oily rag that it wasn't hard, even in a country that surely hit the top spot on every cost of living list. As we had discovered during those first few days, Japan could easily drain your wallet in a very short space of time. Yet here we were putting away around $1,000 a month. It doesn't sound like much these days, but in the mid 1980s it was a veritable fortune to us, and the means to spend another 12 months on the road.

I became a supermarket scrooge. When I cruised the aisles of the local *Daiei* or *Yamazaki* supermarket, my first concern was price. If it cost ¥300, it was too expensive for us. There wasn't much that cost less than ¥300, but that was my rule of thumb. On all our travels through a stream of foreign lands, I'd always found that being able to ask (and understand) prices in the local lingo was one of the most valuable

A Yen for Savings

skills you could learn. And nowhere was this truer than in Japan. I became fluent in supermarket Japanese very quickly.

Since every self-respecting housewife shopped for groceries fresh every day, there was no need for pesky trolleys. And no room in the aisles for them either. You couldn't afford to fill one up anyway. We made do with small but serviceable plastic baskets.

If you were desperate, and there were occasions where that description could have been appropriate, you could eat your way around the store and exit feeling quite sated without having bought a thing. There was no shortage of men and women standing around dishing out samples of the latest delicacy to hit the shelves. They cooked it right there in front of you and encouraged passersby to taste test. Some of the items they offered on the end of toothpicks or in foam trays may have been alien and unidentifiable, but there was plenty of choice.

Another bonus for the non-discerning, supermarket-trawling *gaijin* palate was borne of the Japanese desire for bread without crusts. Unlike at home, they had made a perfect, pre-sliced convenience out of the humble loaf. Bread was sold by weight, around ¥350 for the equivalent of about half a regular loaf, packaged by number of slices. You could buy sandwich slices (twelve to a package), toast slices (either eight or six to a package) or doorstop slices (four to a package). Then there were similar crustless varieties available in all package sizes. But what did they do with all those crusts? The pieces they sliced off each end of the loaf were called *mimi* (ears) and discarded.

Asking for a bag of *pan no mimi*[1] (literally ears of bread) always elicited an embarrassed giggle from the bakery staff. I would bet my shirt on the fact that no Japanese had ever asked for a bag. But though they might have thought us strange, or poor, we were never denied. And for ¥20 you got a whole loaf of end crusts, some often as thick as the doorstop slices that cost more than ten times as much. The only downside was the amount of wax contained in these end pieces, which was used to make it easier to get the loaves out of the tins. But, hey, put together a slice of *mimi* with butter, tomato, and a good dollop of

Kewpie mayonnaise and you couldn't tell the difference. The price was definitely right, so it was a *gaijin* house staple.

Because we were vegetarians, I also quickly learnt how to communicate the concept to would-be profferers of supermarket freebies. "*Saishokushugi desu.*"[2] always met with the same polite response, "*Ah so desu ka?*"[3] and a slightly disbelieving smile. It solved a lot of problems and saved me from having to accept some of the strange and mysterious concoctions I was offered. It only became difficult to explain when I was asked whether I could eat sushi. To the Japanese, sushi automatically implied fish, which I professed to dislike. But there were plenty of vegetarian alternatives — *daikon*[4], *kombu*[5], *natto*[6] (definitely an acquired taste), *kyuri*,[7] and my particular favorite, *ume-shiso*.[8] And I loved them. I quickly became fluent at ordering sushi and was a regular lunch-time customer at the sushi counter in the local Box Hill, a strangely named department store that sat atop Matsudo train station.

I also established a friendly rapport with the lady who worked in the organic fruit and veggie section of the local Isetan department store. The prices were exorbitant, but what wasn't. Better to be poor and healthy, than poor and sickly. The financial outcome was the same either way.

Then there was the local *tofu-ya*.[9] I was there every afternoon ordering two or three blocks of the freshest, sweetest tofu on the planet and a couple of pints of soymilk. Rubber-aproned women with hands red from spending too long in water fished the soft white blocks out of huge stainless-steel baths and packaged them to perfection.

Packaging was another Japanese art form. Every customer service assistant could gift wrap any item you purchased using the smallest viable piece of paper and only one piece of sticky tape. But sometimes it was over the top. I always threw the bakery girls into a spin by asking them not to wrap my pastries in plastic, paper, and then plastic again. They would stop mid wrap, unsure of what to do next. Though childish of me, I found it amusing.

I bought a big piece of disgustingly indulgent chocolate cake on the way home from shopping one afternoon. It had been a hard day, but I did have a tiny space left in the top of my backpack. After I paid for it, I wondered whether I would actually just have cocoa by the time I got it home. But the lady at the bakery was very kind and went to the trouble of packing it in dry ice for me, standard service for anyone who purchased ice cream or frozen goods. She suggested it should ride okay like that on the back seat. I agreed with her, only I'm sure she meant the back seat of a car. What kind of moron would get around on a bicycle in this heat?

I spent the first year of our life in Japan trying to break down walls of stereotypes. I had never fit nicely into a box with a label, even in Australia, and that wasn't about to change just because I'd taken up residence in a foreign country. So, even though we lived close to the throbbing metropolis that was Tokyo, we were something of a novelty in the local area. The only other foreigners we knew for the first 12 months were the ones we'd gotten to know during our time in the *gaijin* house and some of the teachers from James' school. Whenever we were out in public, we were fair game for the tribes of locals who wanted to touch Mani's golden hair, or toddlers who pointed at us and intoned, "*Gaijin! Gaijin!*" over and over, or worse, burst into tears at the sight of us. It was a reinforcement of my firm belief that children learn what they live. How else could such narrow attitudes be explained in ones so young?

The Japanese people I met and conversed with on a very limited basis seemed convinced that no foreigner could ever understand 'We Japanese' or their ways. Admitting to liking *natto*[10] was a favorite stereotype smasher, which always caused them to suck in most of the surrounding air and say, "*Honto?*"[11] as if that could not possibly be true. *Natto* certainly took some getting used to and wasn't for the faint hearted. The smell was bad, like dirty socks, and that alone was enough to put you off even trying it. But mixed with a little mustard and soy sauce and eaten on toast, it became one of my favorite snack foods. 'We Japanese' found that very unusual. Apparently, a lot of them didn't like it.

In fact, 'We Japanese' found lots of things about our little family hard to believe, like the fact that we had moved to Japan with no plan, no jobs, nowhere to live, no knowledge of the language, and with just two backpacks and a baby under 12 months old. I'm sure they thought we were positively certifiable; most of our family in Australia did too. I enjoyed shocking them with tales of our travels and offbeat lifestyle. It helped me to validate the choices we had made, were still making, and had yet to make. Though I can't say they agreed with us on any level, it spoke to my self-esteem in some strange and twisted way.

At first, I used to cringe when 'We Japanese' headed up a sentence that would undoubtedly undermine my feeling that I was actually part of this community. But I grew to love it because it offered another opportunity to show that I really did get it, that I was more than just a foreign face. A lot of the customs and principles that underpinned Japanese society were not only eminently understandable, but also quite sensible and admirable; the little things, the minor details, like taking your shoes off at the door, or washing and showering before getting into the bath, or conducting all official business using a *hanko*. Being *gaijin* offered us the luxury of making a choice about which ones to incorporate into our lifestyle and which ones to avoid, without the attendant social judgment bestowed on Japanese citizens who might want to make similar choices. As *gaijin,* we appeared to be in a category of our own.

12

HOUSE HUNTER

*A*fter almost six months, we had settled in quite well to our new surroundings and worked out a lot of the rules for living in Japanese society and the *gaijin* house. But the stress of living in an international microcosm was beginning to take its toll. While preparing a late-night snack, I happened to overhear a conversation that was taking place in the TV room directly above the kitchen where I was working. Ignoring the toaster that was beeping the completion of its task, I rushed outside to stand beneath the window and get a better handle on what was being said. It was a discussion between several members of the house about my son. I raced back inside and upstairs to our room, where James was getting changed, having just arrived home from a class.

I raced up to our room and summoned him. "Quick, come downstairs. You have to hear this!"

"What? What's happened?"

"Just come with me. Hurry. They're all in the TV room talking about Mani and how they should discipline him." I blurted it all out in shock. It was obvious everyone had had to make adjustments to allow for a baby living in their midst, but until then I hadn't considered the ramifications of living in such a diverse group of adults. For us or for him.

James and I stood under the second-floor window and listened for quite some time. There were a lot of different opinions on how to raise a child, and none of them aligned with our own rather unusual beliefs. We had read and absorbed the controversial ideas of Joseph Chilton Pearce in his books, *Magical Child* and *Magical Child Matures*. We preferred to allow Mani to experience everything without attaching our own negative views to it; we wanted him to learn to draw his own conclusions. Perhaps he was still too young to understand, but he would begin to understand good and bad from his own perspective. None of the others living in the house had children of their own, and most of them had little experience with kids at all. We had put them in the position of having to deal with it without considering the impact. In hindsight, it was a reasonable discussion for them to have, but my initial and perhaps naive reaction was one of surprise.

"We have to get our own place," I said. "We can't stay here." James agreed. It meant a whole new level of interaction with Japanese society and taking on difficulties we couldn't even imagine, but if we wanted to raise our child our own way, with our own set of values, we had to move on.

Never one to let the grass grow under my feet, once the decision was made, I went straight into action. A trip down the local main street revealed that there were only a couple of real estate agencies close by, so with no idea of how to choose between them, I simply chose the first one I came across and fronted up with Mani on my back.

The office wasn't large. Three women seated behind large, paper-covered desks all turned and stared at me, not quite open-mouthed, but the looks of terrified concern on their faces told me they were panicking internally. If I were psychic, I would probably have read these words in their minds: *Oh my God. A foreigner. What on earth could she possibly want?*

"Does anyone speak English?" I didn't even try to mutilate their native tongue. The conversation would have just escalated to a full-blown

Japanese exchange. The Japanese were funny like that. Once you spoke even one word of their language, they obstinately refused to admit to speaking yours. They immediately assumed, wrongly, that my Japanese would be better than their English, and so, to avoid loss of face, they stayed with their own language. It never went well and led to a lot of misunderstandings and resorting to sign language. I desperately tried to hide the fact that my legs were about to fold up in fear and to override my inclination to flee immediately.

The woman at the rear of the office, a classic beauty with an air of coiffured elegance, stood up, straightening her pencil-pleated skirt as she did so. "Yes, but only a little," she said in halting English.

"I'd like to rent a house." Blank faces. I decided to try out the few words I knew that related to what I was after. *"Ie, yachin, dekimasu ka?"* which roughly translated to, "House, rent money, can I?" Far from eloquent, but she got the idea. I could tell this was going to take some time, but they were so patient, once they got over the initial shock of a disheveled foreigner with a baby standing in their office.

As it turned out, she had just what I was looking for, and for only ¥36,000 a month ($360), less than we were paying for a single room with a cupboard at the *gaijin* house. It was still small, just two rooms, a kitchen, and a Japanese style bathroom and toilet. But it was convenient, affordable, and available. Her biggest concern was the fact that I wouldn't be able to use the squat toilet. I fervently wished that I had been able to explain why that was not going to be a problem. If only she knew the half of it. We were gone from the *gaijin* house within a week.

Living in our own place was liberating. And lonely. James was working long hours, commuting all over Tokyo to various Berlitz schools from morning till late at night. Apart from the days we were able to catch up for his lunch break, I spent most days alone with Mani. I missed the long, late night conversations and discussions in the communal dining room at the *gaijin* house. I missed the shared intelligence on places to see and things to do. Once again, we were forced to live by our own wits, finding things out for ourselves, often the hard way.

The bikes were invaluable in our exploration of our new neighborhood. Far from just getting from home to the train station, or doing the shopping, they helped us find various places of interest. Temples, local swimming pools, obscure retail outlets, and crazy, tiny playgrounds with swings and climbing frames. My new best friend, Yuko, introduced me to the best local fruit and veggie shops and the cheapest supermarkets in our area. She was a vital source of information in the early days, and since her English was far superior to my Japanese, she frequently acted as translator on our shopping expeditions. I learnt a lot about how to live like a Japanese from her. I came to understand that it wasn't easy. Or straightforward.

She patiently explained some of the more complicated Japanese customs, like when to use the word *sumimasen*[1] — all the time; when and how deeply to bow; the politics of gift giving or *presento*[2] mania. The Japanese had turned the giving and receiving of presents into an art form, and one not easily understood by hapless foreigners. There were strict rules around gift-giving, and department stores devoted entire floors to gifts for every possible occasion: gifts to give when visiting someone's home; gifts for the boss at bonus time; gifts to thank someone for a kindness; gifts for special holidays; gifts to give as an apology for an inconvenience; gifts to give as a reward for finding a lost item; the list was endless. When we moved into our little house, we had to give a small gift to every one of our neighbors to apologize in advance for any noise we might make or inconvenience we may cause simply by being there. If you had a piano amongst your home furnishings, the gift had to be much more substantial, but usually a cake of soap or a small hand towel would suffice. There was even a law mandating the value of the reward to be offered to someone who found your lost items.

The prospect of visiting the neighbors with a gift filled me with dread. My Japanese was still effectively useless, and I always felt so thoroughly inept in social interactions with the Japanese. They had the benefit of a lifetime of indoctrination in proper etiquette. I had nothing to compete with that. Most of it was a mystery to me and I felt like a klutz. But the Japanese were gracious, and though they may have giggled behind the hands that covered their mouths when they laughed, they were quite forgiving of my foreign imperfections. Still, we did our best to integrate the customs and etiquette of Japanese society into our lives.

13

JOURNAL

September 17

So, we no longer live at the gaijin house. It was a fairly rapid departure, but a move we should have made a long time ago. We have our own house now, only about five minutes by bicycle from the old haunt, but worlds away in atmosphere. The effects of 18 people of different nationalities trying to share a small space, a few of them not of a mind to share anything, were beginning to become unbearable. It was a bad atmosphere for Mani, too, with people constantly telling him not to touch this, and not to do that. The poor child couldn't do anything, and his frustration was turning into biting and nagging. We are all the better for having left the international tension behind.

So, about our new place. It's a classical Japanese-style house, very old, with tatami floors and sliding paper screens. We have one six-mat and one four-and-a-half mat room, not including cupboard space. The kitchen is only three mats (wooden floor) and we have a traditional Japanese bath and toilet. It's cozy. The manager let us bring our futons from the gaijin house and also any crockery we cared to take from the storeroom. He must like us, as everyone else who has tried to take things from the house has faced a deluge of abuse and criticism. We found a nice china cabinet on the gomi last week. Wheeling it back home in the dead of night on the back of a bicycle was interesting. We're now on the lookout for a fridge, a coffee table, an iron, a toaster oven, etc., etc., etc. I've no doubt that sooner or later they will turn up on some likely pile because we did find an electric rice cooker last week.

The rent here is ¥36,000 per month compared with ¥46,000 at the gaijin house, but on top of that we have to pay for gas, electricity, and water, which will just about make up the difference. There is a phone, but the cost of connecting it is extraordinary. And I thought Telecom had sky-high rates. NTT, the Japanese equivalent, charges ¥80,000 (about $800) just to buy the number and the phone line. It's refundable after ten years if you disconnect. Whoopee! I don't think we'll bother getting it connected.

The landlady seems nice. She lives next door in a huge house with her hubby and two kids. The agent I went through to get the place was also friendly and helpful and has since become my student; as of tomorrow, I start teaching her English for ¥2,500 per hour, not bad for just having a conversation. I've asked her to come at 3 p.m., as that's when Mani usually sleeps. I'll have to keep him awake until 2 p.m. to ensure some peace and quiet. She doesn't mind Mani being around, but is a very keen student and, of course, doesn't want to waste time.

My friend, Yuko, and her husband have gone guarantor for us on the house. It was extremely fortunate for us that they were agreeable and there was no hesitation on their part. The Japanese are very generous people on the whole. I have to admit, if a real estate agent that I didn't know rang and asked me to be responsible for the rent for a couple of foreigners I barely knew, I would have to think about it. But everyone couldn't have been nicer to us, and now it feels like we really live in Japan.

We have to give the immediate neighbors a small present for our arrival, kind of a housewarming in reverse, but I'm still working on the Japanese I need to get my message across. "Konnichi wa. I'm your new next-door neighbor. Blah, blah, blah." Should be an interesting exchange. The Japanese have a penchant for giving presents when they visit each other and though there are plenty of shops that sell gifts solely for this purpose, it's always the same old things: cookies, cakes, and Japanese sweets. It would be nice to have some Australian *souvenirs. Koalas are very popular, maybe some chocolate molds of Australian animals that I could use to make some handmade chocolates; one of those coffee table books with photos of our famous landmarks. Might have to ask Mum to send some things over.*

∼

14

HOME VISIT

We got the chance to put the *presento* tradition into practice when one of James' students invited us to their home for lunch followed by an afternoon of tea ceremony and *koto*[1] playing. I went into panic mode wondering what the hell I was going to be able to offer this well-to-do couple in the way of a gift. The woman's husband had studied in the USA and lived in Texas for 15 years. I imagined they had all kinds of foreign trinkets and mementos. What could I possibly give them?

Australia in general, and koalas in particular, have always been popular with the Japanese but it just seemed a little too kitsch to me. I wrote home for ideas and had my mum send over a coffee table picture book and a couple of linen tea towels. But when they arrived, the tea towels seemed so inadequate they ended up in my own kitchen. The book, on the other hand, was quite impressive so it was just going to have to do.

Sato-san and her husband lived out in the suburbs, even further out of Tokyo city than we were. It took a couple of different colored train lines to reach the nearest station and when we arrived, we were surprised to find ourselves more or less in the countryside. The houses were dotted around the landscape rather than huddled on top of each other and they were connected by narrow thoroughfares that skirted an abundance of rice paddies. There was nary an apartment block in sight.

Our hosts kindly collected us from the station and drove us to their home. The house was quite imposing, with far and away the biggest back yard of grass I had seen since our arrival in Japan. Many houses in Japan were two-story by necessity, so they took up less space on the ground. But this one, though an older, traditional-style wooden building, seemed to reflect a position of some status within the community.

We removed our shoes in the *genkan* and stepped up into our first ever 12-mat *tatami* room. The house had recently been updated inside and was a curious mix of eastern and western styles. As I had expected, Sato-san's husband's time in the States was well-represented by lots of souvenirs and curios from those days. I quickly scanned the room for fragile items that Mani might accidentally break but was relieved to find Sato-san had already tucked them safely away in several glass-fronted cabinets that lined the walls. They had no children of their own so were likely unused to the antics of a rambunctious toddler.

"*Dozo*.[2] Please sit down." Sato-san's English was halting and heavily accented, but perfectly correct. It was an easy sentence to string together, but I knew that many of James' students were complete beginners.

There was a large *kotatsu* set in the center of the room. This coffee table-cum-lower body heater was a common item of furniture in Japanese households during the winter months. Even in November, it was a welcome sight. In more extravagant rooms they were often set over a purpose-built hole in the floor allowing those seated around the table the comfort of not having to sit cross-legged. This wasn't one of those, but with little furniture in our own home, we were quite accustomed to living on the floor. We settled ourselves into armchairs without legs and folded ourselves underneath the table and warm blanket.

Sato-san disappeared into the kitchen and returned with a plate of *osembei*, a kind of savory rice cracker, and cups of green tea. I couldn't say that the conversation flowed easily, but the Sato's were kind and very pleasant, and as curious about our foreign lifestyle as we were about their Japanese one. I got the feeling that it had been a long time since they had entertained *gaijin* in their home, and they'd probably never met any quite as different from themselves as we were.

Mani was well-behaved at first, subdued perhaps by the strange surroundings and strained interactions. When he did find his form, he promptly broke one of the precious cups that had been set aside for our tea ceremony experience later in the afternoon. Sato-san was very gracious about the accident, but she was clearly disappointed, and I could not apologize enough. Throughout our time in Japan, I always felt that I lacked the ease of social grace with which the Japanese seemed to be imbued. I often felt socially inadequate, like a proverbial bumbling *gaijin*, adept only at causing myself further embarrassment rather than capable of defusing a difficult cross-cultural faux pas.

In fact, we all committed our own version of a cultural gaff during our visit. Mani broke the teacup. James referred to one of the local festivals incorrectly, which was more funny than bad form. But I took home the prize for the biggest blunder of all. I ate the lunch decorations.

Sato-san had gone to considerable trouble and effort to present our lunch attractively in beautiful, black lacquerware boxes. The steamed vegetables were artistically arranged on a bamboo mat to one side of the tray; there was a small china bowl of thin soup; the chopsticks rested on a miniature carved turtle; the rice was carefully molded into the shape of a fish. And in the bottom right hand corner, three variegated maple leaves trailed delicately towards the edge of the box. It was a work of art.

Being the end of fall, or autumn as we know it in the southern hemisphere, the country was awash with leaves from the omnipresent Japanese maple trees. It was a sensational season and had become one of my favorites, right behind the cherry blossoms. As Australians, we were unaccustomed to this fourth season, when leaves change color, fall from the trees and create a dry brown carpet on the edge of winter. Finding them on my lunch tray, I assumed they were edible. And, so as not to appear rude, I ate them, along with everything else on the tray.

The leaves were neither tasty nor easy to eat. In fact, it was only when I was munching my way through the last of them that I caught the look on my hostess' face. She quickly averted her gaze, but not before I had time to notice and realized, with nothing short of horrified shame, my massive error of judgment. Seeing her face was one of the only times during our stay that I thought there might actually have been some truth to the belief that the Japanese were inscrutable. It showed a mixture of horror, disbelief, disdain, and concern in almost equal parts. Of course, she said nothing, and pretended that nothing unusual had happened. I dearly wished I could hide under the *kotatsu* blanket. James did his best not to laugh out loud. The rest of the meal was uneventful. Apart from the leaves, the food was home-cooked heaven.

After clearing away the dishes, Sato-san returned in a stunning kimono and began preparations for our tea ceremony. The traditional *chanoyu*[3] ritual is like a meditation and can last up to four hours. Strict rules and behaviors govern the proceedings for both participants, from the wiping of the teacup by the server to the way the recipients admire it. However, it is usually not performed in the presence of a toddler, so thankfully, we witnessed the shortened version.

I can appreciate the beauty of a hand-painted porcelain cup with the best of them, but for me, sweet tooth that I am, the tea ceremony has always been about the sweets. The tea itself is an acquired taste, especially the thick variety that is served first. But the intricately decorated sticky rice treats that accompany it (and help to lessen the bitter aftertaste) are to die for. I've even been known to buy them just for the sake of admiring (and eating) them but they are kind of expensive to be consumed as a snack.

Tea ceremony complete, we were treated to a session of *koto* appreciation. I've always loved the typically Asian tones of the long, wooden, stringed instrument but it was difficult to get an 18-month-old to sit still for it for longer than a few minutes. In Mani's case, it was difficult to get him to sit still for anything for longer than a few minutes. We eliminated the stress of trying to do so by staying outdoors and keeping delicate cultural activities to a minimum. So today had been a learning curve for all of us, in more ways than we might have imagined.

On the way back to the train station we visited the local temple and woodblock print museum for our final cultural experience. Japanese temples are beautiful at any time of the year, but especially exquisite in cherry blossom season, and in fall. Mani tired himself out running amok among the fallen leaves. We tired ourselves out trying to keep him from trampling the manicured stone gardens. The Sato's seemed pleased with our gift of the coffee table book of Australian natural scenery. But then, could we even begin to know what they were thinking?

I can say with some certainty, however, that we were all glad to see the end of the visit.

15

JOURNAL

November 16

It's turning miserably cold here now and today was very grey and bleak. We had to turn the heater on much earlier and riding around on the bicycle was almost painful. I need to get some gloves.

Tomorrow we're having a close encounter of the third kind with one of James' students. She has invited us to her place for lunch, tea ceremony, koto playing, and woodblock print viewing. She lives with her husband and mother-in-law, probably in a mansion, and has no children, so I don't know how she's going to cope with Mani. She looked aghast when James told her he would be accompanying us and promised to remove all breakables as he suggested. I hope she realizes kids can climb. He has a cold at the moment and is cutting four molars all at once, so his behavior is not exactly picture perfect. He gave my student a hard time last week and the lesson was a disaster. I had to refuse her money in the end.

Next day

Well, it's over… we all survived the visit, save for one of Sato-san's prized teacups. It was a little bit abunai (dangerous) at times but Mani was, by and large, a well-mannered 18-month-old and fortunately, not as outrageous as he can be at home. We had been viewing the whole experience as a bit of a hassle, but it was nice to see how the other 99.99% live. Sato-san and her husband are mid-40s, and quite well-to-do. They certainly have the largest back yard I've ever seen in Tokyo. The house itself is two-story, as are most Japanese houses, mostly for space economy rather than added size. It was quite old and wooden but had been updated inside. They have a mixture of Japanese and Western styles, which seems a bit eclectic, but her husband did live in the USA (Texas) for several years while he studied. He's been back in Japan for 15 years now and had obvious difficulty remembering any English.

We had a lovely Japanese lunch of hot thin soup and cold steamed veggies served delicately in a black lacquer wood box. Being fall, the whole arrangement was decorated with leaves from the garden. My big faux pas of the day was to eat them. James' was to call the children's festival shichi-gohan (seven meals) instead of shichi-go-san (7 - 5 - 3). Mani's was, of course, breaking the china cup. So, we all had a turn at playing the barbarian.

Our hosts also took us to the city museum to see some magnificent woodblock prints and then to their local temple. It was so beautiful with all the trees changing colors and dropping their leaves. Japanese architecture seems particularly compatible with the fall and winter seasons.

At the end of the day, they drove us back to Matsudo where we'd left our bicycles and we bowed profusely for their hospitality. I always feel more than a little inept when I interact with the Japanese in a social situation. Their customs are so delicate and unobtrusive, like their manner, and being generally larger in size is only the beginning of our problems. They call it tatami consciousness — the art of living in a very small space, something we Westerners find difficult to appreciate. But after you've been here for a while, coming to terms with it certainly has its advantages. There just isn't much space.

~

1986

16
JOURNAL

January 13

We are finally leaving Japan. We've been here ten months, though in retrospect, it doesn't seem nearly so long. James finishes work on January 24, and we fly out to Hong Kong on the 29th. The school seems disappointed that he is going, and they've told him he's welcome back any time. We've saved a lot of money here and it seems like the right time to call it quits. It's not easy living in Tokyo, and it does funny things to you if you stay too long.

I'm not quite sure how I feel about Japan after all our experiences. I think I've tried to adapt to the different social norms of the society over the last year but it's not easy. There are strict rules of etiquette, and you are generally expected to follow them. For a beginner, it takes time to learn the things that locals just know innately. Added to this is the inescapable fact of your foreignness, which seems to keep you at arm's length. It can be very frustrating. I don't want to become Japanese, but I do want to feel I have contributed in some small way, not just come, taken the money, and run.

So, for now we're going to relax for a while on a beach in Thailand and then do some more traveling. Mani needs some space, James needs to forget about work, having done 60 hours a week for the last eight months, and I need some time for me. Mani is very active and very demanding, like any 18-month-old. It will be heaven for him to have all that lovely unbreakable space to run around in, for both of us. James may work 60 hours a week, but sometimes I feel like I work 160.

There's not much packing up to do. Since everything came from the gomi, it's all going back there. One of James' workmates is taking the fridge, air pot, and rice cooker. He's been here 18 months and still doesn't have those necessities. Admittedly, in winter you don't need a fridge. The ground outside our front door is one-and-a-half-inch thick ice at the moment.

Two weeks later

We left Japan last Monday after delaying our departure a number of times. We went to Yatsugatake Highlands for a weekend with friends from Berlitz. We had such a great time that we decided to go skiing with them the next weekend in Niigata, right in the mountains. There was 12 feet of snow on the ground, a sight I'd never seen before, and just beautiful. We did only a little skiing (if you can call it that) on the beginner slopes outside the hotel on Saturday because we slept in, but I quickly discovered how difficult it is. Being able to water ski is no help at all. It's a completely different medium, and oh, so slippery. Mani had a ball, all wrapped up in a very large parka and, toddling around in the snow, looking just like an over-sized penguin.

On the Sunday we took the rope way to the summit and tried to learn to ski on 45° slopes — at least, that's how it seemed. Yuichi is a very skillful skier, so he put Mani on his back and took off down the mountain sans ski poles before I could protest. James followed him despite this also being his first time on skis. It was terrifying to watch him plummet towards the bottom of the mountain in a straight line.

That left me with no option but to follow, but I could scarcely stay vertical and had a number of spread-eagled spills. Lorraine did her best to help, even standing on my skis at one point so that I could get back up from a fall. It didn't work. At least snow is somewhat softer than water. In the end, there was nothing for it but to admit defeat and take the ropeway back to the bottom and wait in the coffee shop for everyone else to arrive. But even at that they all beat me there.

Journal

We moved out of the house on the 29th and into Yuichi's apartment. We got back from Niigata just in time to take a bath, cook lunch, pack, and leave. They drove us to the airport, which is about 90 minutes by car from Tokyo. It was a sad departure for us after so long there, and now we miss it. There was a time when I thought I couldn't get out of Tokyo quick enough. And it's not Tokyo that's endearing. It's the... It's the... Well, I'm not exactly sure what it is. Hong Kong has nothing on Tokyo. The shopping was better, and the people were friendlier, even when they couldn't speak a word of English.

We're flying from Hong Kong to Kuala Lumpur on Saturday. It's the only flight we can get on without waiting here for nearly two weeks. Next Sunday is Chinese New Year and it's busy, busy, busy. Kuala Lumpur via Manila was available for Saturday, so we grabbed it. We had all our shots in Tokyo, so all we're doing in Hong Kong is getting a Thai visa and some supplies we may not be able to get again for some time. We're looking forward to the beach after all that city.

17

ON THE ROAD AGAIN

*1*986 was another entire year of travel for us, spending the savings we'd gathered after almost a year in Japan. My first book, *Restless: Memoir of an Incurable Traveller*, follows our travels during the year after we left Japan. It is available on all Amazon stores.

We returned to Australia briefly before we returned to Tokyo. It was a flying trip, insisted upon by our parents, eager to see their only grandson. But because we'd been away for most of his young life, they didn't know him at all and didn't cope well with the stubborn, busy little fellow he had become. It wasn't their fault; it was entirely ours, but that didn't make it easier for any of us.

Anyone with children who has lived apart from their parents for a long time will understand how difficult that relationship can be. Those left at home grow closer and those that move away, well, don't. They can become strangers. And that's what happened to us.

Our unusual lifestyle and eccentric belief systems made us hard to relate to. Our uncompromising attitudes didn't help. We spent a stressful six weeks defending how we live and raise our child. Our choices and actions had made us outsiders in our own families. It wasn't any wonder that we couldn't wait to leave again, to get back on the road, where no one knew us, and no one judged us.

So, after disappointing everyone at home yet again, and because we had traveled our way through our savings, we headed back to Japan where we knew we could refill the coffers. And be left alone.

1987

18

THE CYCLING REAL ESTATE AGENT

When we arrived in Japan for the second time, our first thought was to return to the same *gaijin* house we had lived in before, at least temporarily. But, as usual, it was full and carrying a long waiting list. The manager was kind enough to rent us the tool room again for a couple of weeks, but not kind enough to be understanding when we found it difficult to find another place to live. But desperation leads one to do desperate things, so armed only with a photocopied list of useful phrases and a basic understanding of the *kanji* that represented the kind of criteria we were looking for in our new home, I marched into a local real estate office carrying my blonde-haired icebreaker, aka my son.

The licensee, Hasegawa-san, was the owner of a tiny shoe box office on the corner of the main road from Ichikawa to Matsudo. The windowed walls that enclosed his minuscule space were crowded with postcard-sized strips of paper advertising the properties he had available at the time. Everything was in Japanese, of course, either *hiragana*,[1] which I could read quite well even if I didn't understand the vocabulary, *katakana*, which was just a Japanese rendition of the English words, and *kanji*, most of which were on my list. I had learnt to recognize which ones advertised houses (*ie*) and which ones apartments (*apato*). There were a couple of properties listed in the window that looked like they might fit the bill.

Hasegawa-san was more than a little fazed by my sudden intrusion into his real estate cubbyhole but recovered quickly enough when I addressed him in my perfect, opening conversation Japanese.

"*Konnichi wa, Haketto desu. Dozo yoroshiku,*" which literally means, "Hi, my name is Hackett. Please treat me as you see fit."

Because the Japanese language is incapable of finishing any word in a consonant other than 'n', *Haketto* was as close a rendition of my surname as I could manage. My first name had become *Heza*, but no one ever called me that here. I bowed respectfully and pulled the crumpled real estate vocab cheat sheet from my pocket. He was so intrigued by the piece of paper that he spent the next ten minutes silently perusing the contents, periodically looking up at me and saying, "*Omoshiroii, ne!*"[2] over and over.

Eventually, he began asking the questions I was mostly prepared for. The first and most obvious one was, "Can you speak Japanese?" to which I always had a fluent, well-practiced reply. The problem was that it gave the wrong impression.

"*Sukoshi dake, demo benkyo shite imasu, ne.*" (Only a little, but I'm studying.) These few words were burned into my brain and I appeared to be perfectly fluent on the back of that one sentence. Well, that, and the conversation around paying for groceries in the supermarket.

I took an instant liking to the strange, little old man I found myself discussing my life with that afternoon. He had a sweet face and welcoming eyes, once he got over the shock of finding a *gaijin* in his office. I got the feeling he was kind of impressed by my courage in even approaching him, and he made me feel much more at ease than I had been when I pushed open the door and stood his world on its ear.

Between my cheat sheet and the few words I managed to pull out of my brain at the appropriate time, my answers seemed to please him endlessly. He relaxed a little and got up and made us both a brew. He wanted to know where I was from, how long I'd been in Japan, how long I intended to stay, what kind of work my husband did, and strangely, whether I had any Japanese friends. Once again, these were all questions I was familiar with, and I stumbled my way through them. The reason for this last question about my friends had nothing to do with my social prowess, and only became obvious later in our dealings; this was his way of finding out whether I would be able to provide a Japanese guarantor for our lease contract, which was mandatory for *gaijin* trying to rent property.

To their absolute credit and graciousness, my friend, Yuko, and her husband came to the party again. And it speaks volumes to the kindness and generosity shown us by the Japanese we met. Personal relationships, such as the one I shared initially with Yuko, and later my housewife students, were in stark contrast to my general interactions with Japanese society at large. They were the polar opposite of our experience at the airport the day we arrived, when it felt like we were struggling alone in a sea of judgement and self-doubt. On a one-to-one level, they offered an olive branch that allowed me to begin to unravel the two conflicting paradigms that make up Japanese culture – the private face and the public façade.

After a respectable amount of time spent on pleasantries, we finally got around to the reason for my visit.

"So, what kind of accommodation are you looking for?"

Using the cheat sheet for clarification, I explained in passable Japanese that we preferred a house with at least two *tatami* mat rooms, plus a kitchen, and a bathroom. I also mentioned that we didn't mind, and actually preferred, a Japanese-style bathroom. This last fact had to be repeated over and over, as it seemed to be unbelievable. He sat back in his chair, stroked his chin with his hand and kept repeating, *"Honto?"*

I managed to convince him by chanting, *"Hai! Hai! Hai!"*[3] at regular intervals, to which he replied, *"Sugoi yo!"*[4]

Finally, he picked up the phone and made a quick call, presumably to the owner of a suitable property, because immediately after, he mumbled something about a bicycle, and I was shepherded outside.

As it turned out, he didn't have a car, and we both got on our two-wheeled steeds and headed down the hill towards the river to inspect the said property. I only gleaned all this from the actions he took as we left his office; not one word had I understood when he explained it to me. He only had one property to show me, but it was all I needed to see.

19

THE LITTLE HOUSE IN THE CABBAGE FIELDS

The little brown house with its grey-tiled roof stood out on its own, looking as if it had been dumped from the heavens into the middle of a market garden. It had a strange, added-on room at the front, which jutted out from the rest of the house. Hasegawa-san explained to me that in a previous life this room had been a small shop, capturing its clientele from the swarms of students passing by on their way to the high school at the bottom of the street. I say street, but it was little more than a narrow track of asphalt through the middle of the fields. My guide had a brief conversation with two tiny old ladies who were tending to the endless rows of cabbages and leeks surrounding the house. I hadn't noticed them at first, as they appeared to be permanently bent in half at the waist and almost invisible under their huge sun hats.

After leaning his bike up against the concrete block wall that separated the driveway from the garden, Hasegawa-san unlocked the front door and ushered me inside.

Even from my first glimpse, I knew the house was perfect for us. It had a small garden of sorts, minus any grass, and no neighbors bar the landlord and his family, who lived in the ugly, beige two-story house at the back. We entered a tiny pebbled foyer where we removed our shoes before stepping up into a hallway that led into the house proper. The bathroom and toilet were behind a door immediately to the left of the main entrance, which seemed like a strange location. Another sliding door on the right led into the smaller of the two *tatami* mat rooms, which featured a tiny verandah overlooking the barren garden.

At the end of the short corridor, we entered a huge open room with parquetry flooring. The kitchen ran along the back wall of the house to our left, and simply consisted of a sink in the middle of a long bench, with space for a gas burner stove at one end. And very little else. The rest of the room opened into the old shop space, which made it feel luxurious and extravagantly large, even though it was dark and musty. The darkness stemmed not only from a lack of light, but also a lack of light fittings. The walls appeared to have been sprayed with a mixture of some kind of bluish textured material and glitter. I know, it sounds hideous, but I'd seen it adorning the walls of many urban dwellings, so it was obviously the latest fashion when the house had been built, a bit like wallpaper had once been the craze in the West.

Renting an empty house took on a whole new meaning in Japan. Unfurnished houses and apartments were let with little more than a *gomi* chart. No furniture, no gas cooker, no oven, not even light fittings, just outlets in the low ceilings from which they could be plugged in and suspended. When I looked up, I noticed there were strange clips in the ceiling where the light fittings would normally have hung. That was something else the tenant needed to provide. There was, however, a large, imposing chart stuck on the kitchen wall detailing every aspect of the rules regarding *gomi*. Though I couldn't understand any of the writing, the pictograms made the instructions abundantly clear.

The last room, off the other side of the living space, was a massive contrast to the rest of the house. It was a six-mat *tatami* room, light and airy, with windows covering the greater part of the two external walls. It was beautiful, destined to become our main bedroom. I turned to Hasegawa-san, who was following me around, nattering away in Japanese.

"*Ii desu, ne!*" I commented. "It's great, isn't it!" He clearly agreed with me, and grinned proudly, as if he were showing me his own home. I wasn't sure how to say, "I'll take it," in Japanese, but the look on my face must have said it for me. We got the house.

Even though the rent was an unbelievably low ¥46,000 per month (about $460), moving in cost us six times that. First, there was the usual two months' rent in advance, then two months' rent as a bond, also nothing out of the ordinary. But the other two months' rent was key money, a gift to the landlord to say thank you for allowing us to rent your property. And that part was non-refundable. And worse, every time the lease was renewed, another two months' key money had to be paid. By the time we left, eight years later, we had been so grateful to the landlord for allowing us to live there that we had practically bought the house.

20

MOVING DAY

Memories are strange animals. I've always found that the strength of recall of a past event is directly proportional to the strength of the emotion attached to it. Some of the things that are stand-out memories for me have been completely forgotten by the other participants in their creation. For whatever reason, they just didn't have the same emotional impact, either positive or negative, on the others involved as they did on me. Situations that I vividly recall as disappointing, humiliating, embarrassing, or even profoundly moving or joyous don't even exist in the memory banks of those who were also there.

And so, the memory of moving into our little house in the cabbage fields and my first meeting with the landlady was no exception, mostly because of the embarrassment and abject humiliation that accompanied it. The day that we moved from the *gaijin* house to our new place in Nakayagiri was such a fiasco it is indelibly linked to those two emotions. And yet, I often wonder whether the landlady even remembers it.

We didn't have a lot of luggage, certainly far less than you usually think of when moving to a new house. We had no furniture, just a few bags and boxes, and a couple of backpacks. But we also had no means of transport other than our bicycles. So, just as we may have done in the same situation at home in Australia, we decided to call a taxi.

Neither my Japanese nor James' extended to making a booking over the phone, so we engaged the assistance of one of the young Japanese men living in the *gaijin* house. His name was Kenji. He was in the middle of cooking his dinner when I asked him to do me a favor by calling the taxi. He happily obliged, but when it arrived, we weren't quite ready to go, still struggling in and out of the house with all our possessions. Kenji came out to the front gate to help us and explained to the driver that we wanted to go down to the house, which wasn't that far down the road, drop off our luggage, and then return.

The taxi driver was impatient, as all Japanese taxi drivers seemed to be. I could tell by the look on his face that he was unimpressed. Not only were we a poor fare in terms of the cost, he was also pissed about being used as a removal service. He refused to open the trunk for the luggage, claiming it was already filled by the LPG tank. So, I had no choice but to toss a couple of bags through the open rear door onto the lace-covered back seat ahead of me.

Blissfully ignorant to most of what was going down between Kenji and the driver, I climbed in after the bags with Mani and tried to make room for James. But before he could get in, the driver slammed the door shut. I should explain that Japanese taxi doors can be operated by the driver, enabling them to pick and choose their fares. If they don't like the look of you or think the fare is too cheap, they simply won't open them to let you in. Unfortunately for the driver, the already-open door had allowed me to clamber inside, leaving him with little option but to ferry us to our destination. But unfortunately for me, James was left outside the taxi with the money to pay the fare. Then the driver insisted that Kenji accompany us, which he clearly wasn't happy about either. After all, his dinner was probably burning away on the stove in his absence. Without intending to, we had committed an entire series of cultural blunders, upsetting everyone's *wa* yet again. The chaos escalated quickly.

"You've got the money!" I screamed at James through the open window, suddenly in a panic about what was going to happen if I had no means of paying the already disgruntled driver. But James' quick thinking saved me, and he threw his wallet through the open window just before the taxi sped away, leaving him stranded on the street.

Now unhappily planted in the front passenger seat, Kenji prattled away in Japanese. There was a liberal smattering of the phrase *gomen nasai*[1] peppered throughout his monologue. The driver remained silent, but clearly furious as he threw the vehicle violently into every curve and corner.

When we arrived at the cottage, I scrambled to remove myself and the luggage as quickly as I could to avoid further distress. I set Mani down in the gravel driveway hoping he would stay there and not crawl onto the road. At this point, I was so flustered I wasn't sure what I was doing, and it took me a while to find the right key to the front door. Kenji ferried the bags and boxes from the taxi to the door and threw them into the *genkan* of the house, filling it up so that we couldn't have gone inside if we had wanted.

All the commotion in the driveway alerted the landlady to our arrival, and she came running out from her house. She had in her hands a giant brochure, all in Japanese. She was babbling away at me so quickly I had no hope of picking up any random words that may have helped me decipher the content. She had been told that I spoke Japanese, and it now became painfully obvious that I did not. I looked desperately at Kenji.

"What is she saying?" He attempted to look over the brochure she was waving around madly and quickly explained to me that it was for a gas stove. She was concerned that we were moving into the house without any means of preparing dinner. She wanted me to choose a new gas stove right then and there so that she could order it immediately. But the taxi driver couldn't wait. He started honking his horn and screaming at Kenji in Japanese, and even though I couldn't understand him, I knew exactly what he was saying. And that he wasn't being polite. We had no choice but to get back in the taxi, leaving the stunned landlady standing by the side of the road in rather the same state as we had left James several minutes earlier.

Oh. My. God. How was I ever going to live this down, or face her when next we met? What must she have been thinking as we drove away? I for one was in shock, astounded at how quickly the situation had degenerated into such a total debacle. Not to blame the taxi driver entirely, but his screaming impatience hadn't helped one iota.

How very un-Japanese of him, I thought, as if I had any real idea of what it meant to be Japanese. Only much later would I begin to understand that Japanese society revolves around private guilt and public shame, and the avoidance of both. This inauspicious beginning was my first introduction to our landlady, Ito-san the Mrs.[2] I couldn't even begin to imagine how much damage I had done to our budding relationship. Thankfully, I had a little time to work on my *gomen nasai* speech before our paths crossed again. But it was a very long time before I got into another taxi.

21

THE GAIJIN NEXT DOOR

*A*nd so, we became the *gaijin* who lived next door — next door to the Ito family.

I'm not saying we were the best neighbors in the world, or the worst, but I did my best not to let the international side down. When Ito-san the Mrs. finally worked up the courage to make a return visit to our door, I was able to restore a little of her faith that we would be able to communicate on some level going forward, even if the bar had been seriously lowered.

"*Gomen kudasai,*" she called from the doorway. It was the equivalent Japanese phrase for 'Anybody home?', but the literal translation was more like, 'Please excuse me for bothering you.' She had the same huge gas stove brochure in her hands, but this time I was prepared for the topic of conversation. I'd had a chance to expand my vocabulary around the ordering and purchasing of a *gasu renji*.[1] I also had time to get a better look at the pictures of what was on offer. She recommended the one with the fish griller in the center, but not being a fan of seafood of any kind, I declined in favor of a cheaper model.

"*Hai, kore wa ii desu, ne,*"[2] was all I needed to say as I pointed to the most basic model. She filled in the blanks with a stream of words, the only ones which I caught and understood being *niman yonsen en* (¥24,000), obviously the price. The significance of the numbers printed below each of the models pictured had not escaped me entirely, so my choice was based solely on price. Though more than half one months' rent, it seemed quite reasonable compared to the cost of everything else so far. She left much happier knowing that we would be able to cook and eat at home from here on out. And I was also happy that she was going to look after ordering my choice for me. I certainly would never have managed it alone. As I bowed her away, I chanted my thank you over and over; *arigato gozaimasu*[3] was another of the basic but useful phrases everyone knew by heart.

It became obvious early on in our time in Japan that we would spend a lot of time either saying thank you or apologizing, and the language had many different ways of expressing humility or regret over your shortcomings. Being a big and tall *gaijin* with a mindset of vast personal space in a country crowded with petite, organized locals trained from birth in *tatami* consciousness, it made sense to learn the right words. Two of the most frequently used phrases we would learn were *gomen nasai* and *sumimasen,* both universal terms for a whole range of apologies. There were, of course, more and less polite ways of saying the same thing depending on whom you were talking to, whether they were older or younger than you, familiar to you or just a casual acquaintance. It made for plenty of excruciating, and hilarious, faux pas. But as is true when learning any language, there is always more to learn, things that native speakers just grow up knowing.

Ito-san the Mrs. collected the rent from me directly every month. It took me a while to catch on, but she would start to appear in the *genkan* with a small gift in hand a few days before the end of each month, when the rent was due. The first time she came, she would bring me a bar of soap or a small hand towel or flannel. The next day, perhaps a bunch of *negi*[4] or half a cabbage. This was my reminder that it was time to pay the rent. I got a bit cheeky later on in our stay and wondered how long she would continue bringing me gifts if I pretended I had forgotten the rent and failed to hand it over. So, I tested it out once. She came every day for a whole week.

It was probably a bit cruel on my part. Our rent money could well have been her source of housekeeping money. But I never needed reminding to pay the rent. I was forever grateful to her and her husband for taking us on and for offering such a lovely little home at such an amazingly low price. Many of James' fellow teachers were living in city-bound apartments where they had to open a window, stick their heads out and look up at a 90-degree angle to even see the sky and find out what the weather was like that day. And they were paying double or triple what we paid for our little house in the cabbage fields. On a clear day, which admittedly was rare, we could even see Mount Fuji on the western horizon.

The Ito's were a nuclear family — Mr., Mrs., and their two sons, the older of whom we rarely saw, but when we did, he looked like he had no desire to engage us in conversation and scurried through his front gate as fast as he could. The younger one was friendly, and we came to call him *Oni-chan*[5] since most of our conversations with him occurred over Mani's head and were usually about Mani, to whom he was like, well, an older brother.

Ito-san the Mr. was more aloof, mostly leaving his wife to deal with the *gaijin*. She was home alone all day. He worked at the local city office, a fact I only discovered accidentally when I happened to run into him while visiting the office to renew our Alien Registration cards. Yep, that's right. We were card-carrying Aliens, just as the sign at the airport had described us on the day we arrived. Anyone staying in Japan longer than 90 days was obliged to register with the local city office, carry the card at all times, and produce it on demand to anyone who asked to see it, even regular members of the public. Back in the day, obtaining one required the taking of fingerprints, just in case you turned out to be a criminal and committed heinous crimes, I guess. The world we live in today is much more aware of and concerned about terrorism, so fingerprinting foreign arrivals has become par for the course, though I believe it's no longer required for Aliens in Japan. But back in the 80s, as honest, law-abiding citizens just looking to immerse ourselves in the culture by living and working in the country, we were mildly offended by the practice.

That's not to say that the people who worked in the city office were unfriendly towards us. Quite the contrary. They always welcomed us. We were regular visitors because, apart from renewing our Alien status every so often, the office was also the seat of power of the baby health nurse and dispenser of infant immunizations. The Japanese immunization regime was a little different to the one we were used to at the local baby clinic at home, but if we wanted to stay on the right side of the law in Japan, we had to present our toddler on schedule to have him jabbed and his shot recorded on his own Alien Registration card.

Our little house was unusual for a Greater Tokyo address in that it stood slap bang in the middle of acres and acres of market gardens. Our closest neighbors were vegetables. The little old ladies who tended the fields almost daily were bent in half from their lifelong efforts. They grew cabbages and leeks in the neighboring plots on a rotational basis, and a little further from the house, they had quite a lot of rice paddies. The fields were built up about two feet above the road level but with no retaining walls to contain the soil. So, in times of heavy rain, the dirt made its way across the narrow bitumen strip and collected in muddy puddles on either side of the road.

The other downside to living in a market garden was the persistent use of pesticide sprays. We used to call them Agent Orange Days because the odor that permeated our home for hours on end smelled strikingly like citrus fruit. Those were the days I was thankful for the wooden typhoon shutters that adorned all our exterior windows. Closing them made it a bit like living in a cave, but it reduced our exposure to the smell, though probably not the chemicals. Between that and the humongous electricity tower 50 yards down the road, our health likely suffered considerably during our stay in Matsudo. We tried to compensate for that with an organic, vegetarian, and eventually vegan lifestyle choice. It seemed that in the pursuit of cross-cultural understanding there were going to be trade-offs.

22
JOURNAL

February 28

It's been a busy time for us since we arrived, and I feel a bit like an overwound clock. Right now, it's about 11 p.m. and I'm taking a break from unpacking clothes, but James is still in the next room on his hands and knees scrubbing down the dusty, parquetry floor.

We moved into our new house yesterday. It took quite a while to get everything here and we used bicycles, a taxi for the four bags, and later that evening my friend Yuko drove us here in her car while we delivered the heater and a bag of odds and ends. We strapped the futons onto the bikes, along with bags of food, crockery, and a small ironing board. Luckily, the road from the gaijin house to here is completely flat.

We found the house through a sympathetic real estate agent with an office near the gaijin house. My old student from a couple of years ago, a real estate agent herself, tried to help us, but she didn't have anything suitable, so we struck out on our own. Because we were able to communicate our requirements and personal information fairly effectively, the agent assumed, wrongly of course, that we spoke Japanese.

The landlord, who lives right behind the kitchen window, accepted us (being foreigners doesn't usually go in your favor) presumably because of our fluency in Japanese. This led to a few headaches when we had to make arrangements for the delivery of a new gas stove, but today we have successfully negotiated this minor calamity without the gas man even knowing we were non-speakers of Japanese. Wonders never cease! All in all, people have been extremely helpful, which makes the going a lot easier.

The rent is ¥46,000 a month including water. Gas and electricity are extra. That's about $460, which, for its size, is really cheap. Our house and the landlord's stand alone, surrounded on all sides by market gardens. The nearest neighbors are just around the corner. We're about ten minutes from the old gaijin house and ten minutes from Matsudo and James' school. There's a telephone here, but we won't have the money to have it connected for some time. It would probably be cheaper for us to rent than to buy the connection, though they can be bought from other foreigners leaving the country for around ¥65-70,000, a saving of ¥15-20,000.

It's freezing now. There was a light snowfall the other day, and when we arrived there were large patches of ice in the streets. The snow had been heavy just before we got here. The peach and plum blossoms are out already, and the cherry blossoms begin next month. I'm looking forward to that. It's a beautiful time of year.

The poor old Aussie dollar is only worth around ¥100 at the moment, down from ¥180 a couple years ago, so we've given up converting prices because everything sounds so expensive. For example:

- 1 pint (~500ml) of milk = ¥190
- 6 slices of bread = ¥170
- 8 oz (~250g) of whipped margarine = ¥699
- 2 lb. (~1 kg) of muesli = ¥1,000+
- Train and taxi fares from domestic airport to gaijin house = ¥2,500 (not bad considering the above)

We had a Cook's Tour of Tokyo the night we arrived. Coming in on China Airlines meant landing at Haneda Airport instead of Narita. But clearing customs took some time because it was so crowded, and the inspectors were being very thorough. Since Japan recognized the government of China and began diplomatic relations recently, Taiwan's China Airlines is the only international carrier permitted to land at the domestic airport. It's much closer to Tokyo than Narita and the main reason for choosing to arrive there, but it took us a good three hours to reach the gaijin house.

We caught the monorail into the city and boarded a train directly to Ichikawa right in the middle of peak hour. The train became so crowded that by the time we reached our stop, getting off was impossible. The Japanese commuters were not impressed by our voluminous luggage. One girl, crushed against a pole by the crowd, was moaning in pain. I had a seat by the door with Mani on my lap, but James had only toe space on the floor. We went all the way to Chiba City before we could get out, about as far from Ichikawa as Ichikawa is from Tokyo. We crossed the platform, boarded a waiting train, waited for 45 minutes, and then moved off in the same direction. So, at the next stop we had to manhandle all our bags off the train again and try to work out which of the ten platforms would be the right one to take us back to Ichikawa. Welcome back, gaijin.

James starts work on Monday. The school hasn't changed, just added a couple of teachers, but not all of them for English. There are now French, German, and Russian teachers based there. Tomorrow we're going into Tokyo to have dinner with the Japanese American head teacher. It will be only our second trip to Tokyo since we arrived. James went in last week to arrange his contract hours at the Berlitz head office. He's back on the afternoon shift. The salary has gone up a little, and so have the bonus lesson rates, but it's probably just in keeping with the cost of living. Heaven forbid that should have increased.

23

ACCLIMATIZATION

We quickly settled into life in the Japanese 'burbs. Mani and I filled our days with household chores, reading books, and finger painting. He liked to play outside in the garden, which was really just a big patch of dirt. It was a great creative space for him with his cars and trucks when it was dry. But during the wet season (July/August) or any other time it rained, it was a total nightmare.

The lane way that ran past the front of our house was a badly maintained strip of bitumen that led to the middle school, golf course, and tennis courts down on the riverbank. Because of that, it was well used. Every morning and afternoon, hordes of students passed by. Every single one of them knew that a family of *gaijin* lived in our house. I knew that they knew because I could hear the word *gaijin* being bandied about as soon as they turned the corner, 100 yards up the road.

Call me paranoid, but the moment I was alerted to the sound of my generic name floating down the road on the breeze, I would run and scoop Mani up from where he was playing in the garden, draw all the curtains and hide in the kitchen, the room farthest from the front windows. If I failed to get Mani inside in time and he happened to be playing in a puddle of mud, which he often was, I'd hear choruses of *musekinin* from the teenage passersby. I had to look it up in the dictionary to find out what it meant — irresponsible. It was a harsh judgement, and not one of them was old enough to know the first thing about living with a toddler.

From then on, I vowed to avoid the judgmental, dark blue hordes at all costs. Thus, my slightly eccentric behavior when they approached our house. I guess you had to be there to understand why it drove me to distraction, but living through it every day, sometimes twice a day, wore me down. Finally, I insisted that James erect a bamboo fence to provide some semblance of privacy for us, which he did. But it blew down in the first good gust of wind and proved useless.

Ito-san the Mr. must have felt sorry for us and our feeble attempt at building a fence because one fine weekend, he, Ito-san the Mrs. and *Oni-chan* had a working bee in our front yard. We did show up and try to help but we seemed to get in the way more than anything. Mani hung around them all day, driving his cars and trucks between their legs as they hammered and nailed, but they didn't seem to mind. I offered them cups of tea and plates of rice crackers in an effort to appear useful and grateful, but they politely declined. At the end of the day, a much sturdier screen protected us from the prying eyes of passersby. The Ito-sans had done a stellar job.

Since they had gone to so much trouble to improve our garden and, unbeknown to them, our lives, James and I decided to do likewise on the inside of the fence. We visited the local DIY store and purchased rolls of turf, a few fledgling plants, and lots of packets of seeds with which to create our own organic veggie patch. We planted red peppers, basil, parsley, eggplants, and soybeans in the newly dug spaces left by the shrubs. It wasn't a farm, but it helped us to feel that we were taking back a small amount of control over our food supply. We were most pleased with the new lawn and congratulated ourselves on the successful greening of our small plot of earth.

My fellow expat friend Molly came to visit a few days after we had laid the new turf. I made her a cup of coffee then led her out into the garden so that she, too, could appreciate our cleverness. She surveyed our handiwork then asked the inevitable question, the one we hadn't considered, "How on earth are you going to mow it?"

I looked around the yard, stumped. It wasn't a vast area, but there was no way we were going to buy a lawn mower. Neither could I imagine finding one discarded on the *gomi*, at least, not one that worked. "I guess I might just have to cut it with a pair of scissors."

Molly almost choked on her coffee. "Oh, please," she guffawed, "if you do that, make sure you take a photo. Better still, invite me over. I have to see that!"

I couldn't help laughing along with her. The idea of cutting the grass with scissors was indeed ridiculous, but I needn't have worried. The grass never grew. In fact, it died completely just a couple of weeks later, along with most of the plants, whose leaves were stripped by bugs almost as soon as they appeared. I guess that's why we were surrounded by chemical-blown cabbages. The bugs must have thought they had found heaven inside our little fenced enclave.

Partly because we had to abandon our attempt at self-sustainability, we had to find some other way to eat healthily. So, we decided to become vegans. We had been vegetarian since we had travelled around India. So, now we were living in the country that had practically invented macrobiotics, it seemed only natural we should investigate this option.

After thumbing through the classified ads in the back of the *Tokyo Journal*, a magazine popular among the expat community, I found a class teaching macrobiotic cooking techniques. Every Saturday afternoon for six weeks, I travelled across town to the private home of a young Japanese woman who explained the intricacies of preparing healthy dishes and preserving the natural goodness of the ingredients. And at the end of each session, our small group got to share the delicious recipes she had created during the demonstrations.

She not only taught us how to cook great food, and why we should cook it the way she showed us, she also told us where to shop. They were out of the way and difficult to find, but thanks to her classes, I discovered some of the best health food stores in the city. Until then I hadn't believed they existed in this society that appeared to be built on convenience and consumerism.

I also learned a whole new vocabulary and became more confident asking questions about the food I bought. It was hard to get my head around the price tags. Eating organically in Tokyo didn't come cheap. I managed the household on a food budget of ¥120,000 per month (about $1200). At the time, it equaled about one-third of James' entire salary, and since Mani was still largely breastfed, it was really just for the two of us.

One of my favorite shops was the *tofu-ya* in Kitasenju. A couple of times a month, I would ride my bicycle towards the city to a suburb that was about 20 minutes away by express train. It was a bit of a hike, but well worth the trip. Each time I visited, I spent about ¥30,000 on blocks of fresh tofu, soymilk, soy cheese, tempeh, and bags of *kara-age*, battered pieces of deep-fried gluten that resembled and tasted similar to chicken nuggets when cooked.

My other major source of fresh produce was the *saishokushugi-ya* in the basement of the local Isetan department store. That hard-to-say mouthful came to roll off my tongue with ease after a relatively short time. It means 'seller of vegetarianism' and the middle-aged lady who ran it was one of the friendliest salespeople I ever had the good fortune to meet. She always greeted me with gusto, as if I were her long-lost friend. My rudimentary Japanese didn't bother her in the least, and I learned a lot from our short but frequent conversations while I shopped in her little corner of the lower-ground floor supermarket. I may well have been one of her best customers.

The Japanese habit of shopping for groceries every day became my habit too. It seemed more affordable somehow. Although I was always at the market or in the shops, my daily spend was lower. And even though the costs quickly added up, it was easier to pretend not to notice.

A few years later, when my sister-in-law came to visit, she couldn't get over the fact that just a few items in my shopping basket had cost me almost $50. The only advice I could give her was this, "You have to stop converting from yen to Aussie dollars or you're never going to buy anything."

I had come a long way from my initial stance on supermarket prices. When we first arrived back in 1985, I had a price policy, a strategy if you like, that had helped me save a lot of money in a fairly short period of time: if it cost more than ¥300, it was too expensive and I would put it back. Now, just a few years down the track, if it cost ¥1,000, I considered it a bargain and I would buy two. The longer we stayed in Japan, the more money we ended up spending. It was becoming harder and harder to achieve the goal that had brought us to this country in the first place — to save money. The longer we stayed, the longer we had to stay.

Financially, we had acclimatized.

JOURNAL

May 15

So, after a couple of months the house is starting to feel cozy and we've finally got curtains on all the windows. The parcels we posted here ahead of us arrived late last week. There were a few things in them that helped to decorate, plus lots of books I've been looking forward to reading again. Most importantly, we have topped up our stash of Vegemite and Nature's Cuppa.

We've been putting a lot of energy into the house since we moved in, not only putting up a gutter on the verandah to stop the garden from turning to mud in the rain, but also planting a lawn. We've had to dig up the compacted earth and sift out the rocks because otherwise nothing would grow. It's pure rubble out there. The Ito-sans have re-erected our six-foot high bamboo fence, replacing our own paltry attempt at privacy. It blew down shortly after we put it up, taking the biggest tree in the corner of the garden with it. We get lots of wind, being out in the open surrounded by fields, not to mention an inch-thick layer of new dust every time we open a window.

Now that we actually have a garden that's somewhat protected from the wind, we have moved all the shrubs to one corner and planted some herbs, vegetables, and soybeans in the new spaces. But not before we rejuvenated the soil with some steaming horse dung and straw mixture that was kindly dumped across the road at about the same time.

Today we started on the bathroom and painted the ceiling and two of the walls a new color, because mission brown is just depressing. Duck egg blue is much brighter and yes, we do intend to paint the other walls, but we ran out of paint. Mani had a great time helping, but we had a bit of extra cleaning to do as a result; he wanted to paint the floor tiles too and was very proud that he'd managed to get more on the grouting than either of us.

The last three days have been beautiful spring, short-sleeve weather, but today it's rainy and dismal. We have to go out in it, too, to meet James in Matsudo for lunch. Then we're going to buy all the necessary survival rations for an earthquake: water, candles, matches, torches, batteries, and some tinned food spring to mind, but I'm sure there's more. This morning we had the first decent shake since we arrived, about 30 seconds of banging windows, swinging lights, creaking walls, and shaking floorboards. That's jolted us into action.

Tokyo is definitely living under the threat of the Big One. It seems there are two sources of stress, one in the ocean off Shizuoka caused by the shifting continental plates, and the other in the earth under Tokyo itself. There are around 22 different varieties of soil under the city and it operates like a giant bowl of pudding, extending to a depth of a couple hundred miles and containing a good sprinkling of active faults. Quakes from this source are more concentrated and hence, more dangerous and unpredictable. They hope to have from 48-72 hours' warning of an oceanic quake, but they may not get any notice at all from an urban one.

Two things that might save us is the fact that there are no buildings close by, and we are very close to the river. The authorities expect a huge percentage of fatalities to be caused by falling glass and other heavy objects. It's a possibility we all have to live with. Better to be prepared, but I think we'll be okay here.

On a lighter note, we spent the weekend cherry blossom viewing. The rain today will probably spell the end of them, but they were exquisite. We rode our bikes to a suburb of Matsudo, about 45 minutes away, where there is a two-mile-long roadway lined by cherry blossoms forming an archway over the street. The road was lined with festival stalls selling all sorts of souvenirs and special festival snacks and sweets. One section was crammed with spectators watching about 100 tiny women dancing in formation in matching blue and white kimono with bright pink sashes. They were all only about five feet tall.

Then on Sunday, we crossed the river near our house and found a temple full of spring flowers and, leading up to it, another street full of stalls and craft shops. It was a weekend of fascinating finds. It's one of the things I love about living here, how easily and unexpectedly we come across uniquely Japanese customs or events while we're just roaming around the streets on our bicycles.

We're going to get the phone connected at the end of the month. We've waited several months to begin the process because it's so expensive and a bit of a commitment. First you have to buy shares in NTT, the local phone company. That costs ¥72,000 and entitles you to a phone number. Then there is an ¥8,000 connection fee regardless of whether you already have a line in the house or not. If you don't have a phone, you can either rent one from NTT or buy one for about ¥7,000. We do have a phone here, but we still have to rent it for around ¥200 per month. Even local calls are timed and cost ¥10 per three minutes. It is possible to resell the shares you have to buy initially for around ¥60,000 in a private sale or ¥40,000 if you sell them back to NTT. So, I guess it's not as bad as it seems. It's just such an enormous outlay upfront, half as expensive as it was to move into this house, which puts it into perspective.

I'm going to get serious about learning Japanese soon. I've been working my way through a book that was designed to be used with a series of local TV shows, but it's so basic it's too easy for me already. I've been in touch with a teacher recommended by a friend and she is going to let me know about lessons next week. I need to take them at a time when James can mind Mani, currently only Monday mornings. We will meet in a coffee shop in Ichikawa. There wouldn't be much point trying to learn the language while chasing Mani around the cafe. I feel as though I could get a better handle on the Japanese language with some serious study. In some situations, understanding only a little is worse than not understanding anything at all.

25

KYOTO BY TRAINS

During our first year in Japan, the main objective had been to save money. So, traveling around sightseeing, spending our hard-earned yen was not high on the agenda. This time around though, we wanted to see as much of the country as we could. Berlitz was accommodating when it came to taking leave, giving James up to three months without pay each year, on top of his two weeks' paid leave. The trouble was, it was always cheaper to leave the country and spend the time anywhere else in Asia than it was to travel around Japan.

There were lots of beautiful destinations in this picturesque country, but none as famous as the ancient capital of Kyoto. Its stunning temples and Zen gardens were legendary, and no self-respecting *gaijin* would dare leave the country without at least one visit. So, I started researching the cheapest way to get there.

The *Shinkansen*, aka the bullet train, was right out. At about ¥15,000 per person each way it was way beyond our meagre budget, even if it did take only four hours from Tokyo. No, if we were going to travel by train, it was going to have to cost less than that.

Having taught myself some of the common Japanese characters that applied to the national transport system, I deduced that it might be possible to take several local trains, one after another, and reach Kyoto in a kind of bunny hop from one city to the next. It would likely take an entire day, but it was going to save a small fortune in train fares. In fact, by happy accident, it ended up costing us only ¥300 each.

I can't say whether the system is still the same as it was when we lived there, but back in the day, the purchase of a ¥120 ticket gained you access to most train platforms. If you weren't sure how much the fare was going to be, it made sense to simply purchase the cheapest option and then pay the balance at the other end. At least if questioned by a guard, you had a ticket and could pay for an upgrade to your destination. We would start from Tokyo and see how far we could get on the slower, local network lines.

Once outside the city limits, endless high-rise apartment buildings, and busy highways gave way to rice paddies and distant mountains. The near-perfect cone of *Fujisan*[1] dominated the scenery and held us spellbound as we headed southwest across the Kanto plain. We'd never seen it from such close range before. It had always been just a smoky outline on the Tokyo horizon. But now we had time to take in the changing landscapes that disappeared in our wake. We also had to be constantly vigilant, referring to the route map to keep track of where we were and how far we had to go before the next change. Sometimes that was easy because the train terminated, but not always. Most legs took somewhere between one and two hours. It was a tiring way to take a fairly relaxing journey, but we never encountered a single guard or conductor and consequently, were never asked to present our tickets.

We spent an entire day on various local trains, leapfrogging our way across the middle of Honshu, Japan's main island. Some of the trains were express and some stopped at every station. We didn't care. Parts of the itinerary gave us just a few minutes to change platforms, while others allowed more than enough time to visit the station kiosk and pick up snacks and refreshments for the next leg of the journey.

When we finally boarded our last train of the day, we were only half an hour from our destination. We rolled into Kyoto in the early evening dusk, admiring a skyline dotted with the silhouettes of exotic eastern temples and concrete boxes. It was an unlikely juxtaposition.

The station was busy, as all Japanese railway stations are in the late afternoon rush. We found a quiet nook in which to plonk down our bags and look for the cheap tickets we had purchased in Tokyo. But they were nowhere to be found.

"Oh God. What are we going to do? How on earth are we going to explain this?" I looked to James for suggestions, but he just shrugged.

"Just tell them we lost them." Apparently, he had already decided that I was going to be the one to deliver the official explanation at the ticket window. Just the thought of it made my knees go weak. I started rehearsing the conversation in my head.

"Right. And what would the word for 'lost' be do you think?" I could feel the sarcasm rising in my throat the way it always did in the face of a linguistic situation.

"Well, ticket is easy. That's just *ticketto*. Maybe just add *arimasen*.[2] That should work." Yes, he was right. That probably would work. But what about the questions that were bound to follow? I'd have to wing it. I approached the ticket window in a nervous state.

"*Gomen nasai. Ticketto arimasen.*" My apologetic declaration was met with an impassive stare from the attendant and a lot of words I didn't understand. Luckily, I did catch two rather important ones that gave me a clue — *Eki*[3] and *kara*.[4] There were a lot of other words in the sentence, but I understood that I was being asked where we had boarded the train. Without thinking, I gave him the name of the station where we had last embarked, the small town only a half hour back up the line.

"*Sambyaku-rokuju en,*" he replied without blinking. (¥360)

I couldn't believe my luck. He didn't even question my reply. I quickly handed over the cash and retrieved the two tickets that spat out of a machine and into the counter tray.

"How much did it cost?" James asked when I returned to where he waited near the ticket barriers with Mani and our bags.

"One hundred and eighty yen each."

"What? How come?" He clearly didn't believe me. I still couldn't quite believe it.

"He asked me where we had come from and I gave him the name of the last station we got on at. That was the fare from there I guess."

It was a massive stroke of luck. We had travelled all the way from Tokyo for the princely sum of ¥300 each, and although it had taken all day, we had made a massive saving, roughly ¥35,000 cheaper than the *Shinkansen*.

Because of the cheap fares, we were able to splurge on an authentic Japanese inn for our first night in town. It would only be for one night and we would have to look for somewhere cheaper in the morning, but our recent home visit notwithstanding, it would be our first taste of true Japanese hospitality.

Our guidebook recommended a small, family-run *ryokan* just a short walk from the station, so we set off on foot in very high spirits.

∼

26

CHRISTMAS IN KYOTO

The little *obasan*[1] who greeted us at the door of the tiny Japanese inn welcomed us enthusiastically. She spoke no English at all, but that didn't deter her from prattling away to the *gaijin* who just barely managed to ask for a room in Japanese. She gestured for us to remove our shoes in the entrance and step up into the plastic in-house footwear, then ushered us upstairs to a traditional *tatami* mat guest room. She explained the features of the room at length, indicating the location of the futon, *yukata*[2] robes, and toweling room slippers. I understood very few of her actual words apart from the tariff, but the meaning of most of the instructions was self-evident.

Lastly, she offered to show us the bathroom, which was back downstairs. We were quite used to the strict rules about ablutions in a shared Japanese *ofuro*,[3] though she had no way of knowing that. Our own little home in Tokyo had a deep Japanese tub in which we all soaked, one after another, till our skin blushed.

This bathroom was much larger than ours but contained the same basic tools and accoutrements. A low shelf by the door held a stack of small white washcloths, and a tiny, wooden stool graced the corner of the tiled room close to the taps and portable shower head. The hot tub took up more than half the space. The idea was to first wash yourself from head to toe, rinse off thoroughly, then slowly lower your sparkling clean, naked body into the steaming tub — emphasis on the word slowly.

The water was so hot it took some time to acclimatize so that you didn't faint on your way down. The tub was deep enough to allow you to sit or kneel comfortably on the bottom and still keep your head above water. But once submerged, it was best to keep movements to a minimum to avoid stirring up the heat. The small square washcloths came into their own here. If you soaked them in cold water first and placed them on your forehead, they did a pretty good job of preventing you from passing out.

The inn boasted two bathrooms, one each for men and women, rather than the traditional mixed bathing arrangements. Though shared facilities still existed in suburban and rural areas, they had become less common in the postwar era, when Japan was largely rebuilt by occupation forces from several western countries. But even though they were single sex use, they were often not private, particularly in *ryokan* and *onsen*.[4] While I relished the experience of the traditional *ofuro*, in such situations I found myself trying to cover a full square yard of bare skin with a few square inches of washcloth while also keeping watch over a toddler who didn't want to get into the hot bath.

We huddled in the doorway of the bathroom while our host rattled on in Japanese, presumably about the ablutions. Not wanting to appear impolite, we said '*Hai*' a lot, and nodded and bowed in the appropriate places. That always seemed to be the right thing to do. But then, who really knew?

Back in our room, we stowed our minimal luggage in the cupboard, dragged out the bedding and made our bed on the floor. The *futon*[5] were much thicker, warmer, and more luxurious than the ones we were used to at home. Ours had been donated by the kind manager at the *gaijin* house but had most likely been another rescue item from the monthly *gomi* raids. Beggars flocking to Japan to make their fortunes couldn't afford to be choosers. Of anything. Not even bedding. *Futon* were outrageously expensive.

The next day, the first item of business after breakfast was to find cheaper lodgings for the rest of the week. Being New Year, the whole of Japan was on the move, so accommodation was thin on the ground. We did manage to find a *gaijin* house in Central Kyoto, and still enjoyed the comfort of a thick futon on the floor, albeit vinyl tiles instead of *tatami* matting. The place wasn't as clean as it could have been, and one person filled the tiny, shared kitchen. But Kyoto itself made up for any lack of luxury.

The scenery, the food, and the temples were all stunning. We idled down the Philosopher's Walk under leafless trees, wrapped in scarves and mittens against the winter morning chill; we discovered and ate numerous boxes of *yatsuhashi*,[6] devoured steaming bowls of *udon* noodles topped with tofu and sticky *mochi*.[7] We visited all the famous temple landmarks, marveling at the exotic shapes and soaring rooflines. *Kiyomizudera*[8], perched high on a hillside overlooking the city, stunned us not only with its views, but also with its architectural engineering.

As I sat in silence at the edges of Zen gardens made of raked stones, I was reminded of my time spent in the meditation center back home. It was also a small window for reflection on how far we had come, and how far we had yet to go. We had come to Japan with a singular purpose – to earn enough money to continue exploring our world. But we had found so much more. Kyoto was our heaven, our respite from the trials of learning the Japanese way. Kyoto simply embodied the Japanese way.

We spent the entire week wandering without aim through Kyoto's narrow backstreets and alleyways, admiring the wooden houses of the Gion[9] district, catching glimpses of a bygone era and the geisha culture. We wore ourselves out while getting to know Tokyo's biggest tourism rival.

When the time came to return home, the prospect of an all-day journey on one train after another didn't sound as much fun as before. Though we still couldn't stretch to the bullet train, we opted for a couple of intercity rapid express trains that got us back to Tokyo in just a couple of transfers. We made it home for New Year.

1988

27

JOURNAL

January 7

Kyoto was just beautiful. We spent the whole of Christmas Day on the train getting there. It took about ten hours and four changes of train, but even the local trains in Japan are comfortable. Changing trains and working out how to negotiate the next station kept us occupied studying maps and trying to decode the Japanese announcements as we reached each train's terminus. Mani travelled well, playing with his nendo[1] and driving his cars up and down the seats, windowsills, aisles, everywhere really, most of the time.

The train line south from Tokyo follows the Pacific Coast, which is quite rugged, especially around the Izu peninsula. I didn't realize how cut off I felt from nature until I saw the ocean again. Living in Tokyo gives you a warped idea of Japan and the Japanese. The people in Kyoto were so welcoming and seemed more relaxed which, in turn, made us feel at ease while we were there. Perhaps it's the strong relationship with Buddhist and Shinto culture that is so evident everywhere in the city.

We spent one night in a traditional Japanese inn, then moved on to a gaijin house in the center of the city, certainly the cheapest place in town, but not necessarily the cleanest. The room was okay, tatami style with futons and a *heater, but the kitchen was a little overused. One person filled it up, but we managed to cook our evening meal in record time and get out before the next crowd of two. At $40 a night it was bedrock prices for Kyoto, where rooms in top class ryokan can cost upwards of $200 per person per night – two meals included.*

Kyoto is littered with temples; we visited all the more famous ones, as well as some that weren't so well known, and some of the surrounding small towns. We also made a day trip to Nara, the ancient capital. The beauty of Kyoto is that although it is a city of considerable size, it is still small enough to be close to the countryside. It's surrounded by mountains within about half an hour's reach. Nara and Osaka are only 45 minutes away by train.

Today has been one of the coldest days of the winter and since it's raining now, we'll probably get some more snow tonight. We've had quite a few snowfalls already, one just before Christmas with snowflakes the size of pennies. Even Matsudo, ordinarily just like any other urban city, looks beautiful in the snow. It seems to make the light much brighter and the air clearer. We have two kerosene heaters to fight the cold, and we've been using them both lately; one in the bedroom and the bigger one in the kitchen/dining room. They're quite effective, and with kerosene at about $1.60 a gallon, they are cheap to run. Five gallons lasts us about eight days of solid use.

Kerosene may be cheap but petrol costs $6.00 a gallon; you do get a full-service driveway experience for that though. While they fill the tank, they also clean the windscreen, empty your ashtray, take out any rubbish, and run to the counter with your cash. Then, when you're ready to leave, they step out into the road and stop the traffic so that you can safely, and speedily, get back on your way. And, they bow as you drive away.

My Japanese has been getting a workout lately. We're having some people come and stay here to housesit while we're away in Nepal. Trying to explain that to the landlady and the estate agent has been taxing. I explained to Ito-san the Mrs. as best I could and asked if it was okay, but after talking to her husband, she asked us to go see the agent. I understood that Ito-san the Mr. was worried about something, but I wasn't sure what. After talking to them both together on Christmas Eve, I got the impression they didn't believe we were going to come back. But I was wrong. He thought that we were all going to live here together when we got back. We were able to put his mind at rest on that count. One of our house sitters is Japanese, so at least they will be able to communicate fluently with her, but we still haven't got the final approval yet. As well as not leaving the house vacant and locked up for three months, it will save us over $1,200 in rent.

28

NEPAL AGAIN

*I*t was only a matter of time before our beloved Nepal called to us again and we felt compelled to answer. The tiny mountain kingdom and its beautiful people had captured our hearts. Though we wanted to see Japan too, it was hard to justify the expense of traveling locally when we could see so much more for so much longer, and for the same money if we headed to South Asia. Thailand, India, and Nepal were strong competition. So, early in 1988, we returned to Nepal via Thailand and Burma.

We booked our onward flights in Bangkok, opting for a Royal Nepal Airlines flight from Bangkok to Kathmandu with a seven-day stopover in Burma. We had specifically chosen to avoid Burma Airways and its poor relation, Biman Bangladesh, two of the cheaper but less desirable carriers. We'd had previous experiences with both that had left us with only one conclusion — never again. But on our arrival in Rangoon, we were informed that the next leg of our flight had been canceled and we had been transferred to a Burma Airways flight. The good news was that this change of schedule meant we were going to get to stay an extra two days in Burma, though we would probably spend that time caught up in the bureaucracy of extending our visas. And that's how we met an American couple, Rosemarie and

Nepal Again 123

Carl. We'd all been caught up in the consequences of the change in schedule.

The flight out of Rangoon was scheduled for early morning, but by the time we arrived at the airport the requisite two hours in advance, it had already been delayed. News had come through that Tribhuvan Airport in Kathmandu was fogged in so there was no point taking off until we could be assured of clearance to land. After waiting a couple of hours, it was decided to reroute the flight through Dacca in Bangladesh. It wasn't ideal, but at least we would be on our way and a couple of hours closer to our destination.

The flight into Dacca was horrendous and left us with no illusions about the skill of our pilot. It was a perfectly clear morning and the airport was visible from miles away, hovering at the other end of the wide flat Ganges delta. From the air, it was an impressive maze of waterways dotted with tiny pockets of uninhabitable land. For some reason, the pilot seemed to find it difficult to manage his airspeed and correlate it with our distance from the airport. The plane's engines slowed, our altitude dropped, then suddenly we sped up again. It was disconcerting, nerve-racking even, but eventually we landed safely in Dacca.

Everyone was herded from the plane and into the airport transit lounge. We had been informed that the airport in Kathmandu was still closed and we had no idea how long we were going to be on the ground here. On our way into the airport lounge, several of the security guards asked us if we had any whisky and cigarettes to sell. Others asked us if we would purchase some at the duty-free store and sell it to them. It sounded like a risky proposition in this Muslim country, and we declined. Plus, we were not going to spend any time in Bangladesh, so we had no use for any Taka, the local unit of currency.

When we finally boarded the plane and took off from Dacca, the captain advised that the airport in Kathmandu was still closed and when we reached Nepal, we would be put into a holding pattern until it was safe to land. This was not a popular decision with most of our fellow travelers. No one wanted to be circling the Kathmandu Valley, surrounded as it was by the highest mountains in the world, with a pilot who struggled to land at an airport with a perfectly flat approach. But that is exactly what happened.

We spent about 45 minutes traveling in tight circles, watching the mountains appear and disappear into thick cloud, each time looking nauseatingly closer than the last, and listening to the engines slow down and rev back up over and over again. It didn't inspire confidence. So, when we finally touched down, there was a collective sigh of relief from the passengers. And then a huge cheer.

Our previous visits had taught us the finer points of avoiding the pitfalls awaiting the unwary just outside the airport doors. So, we considered ourselves dab hands at negotiating the horde of taxi wallahs vying for attention. While waiting for our bags to be ferried across the tarmac, we offered to chaperone Rosemarie and Carl through the rabble and into the city proper. They gratefully accepted and as we wove our way through the outskirts of the city in a giant cream-colored Humber, we watched the looks on their faces with amusement. Nepal had a way of confounding even the most seasoned travelers with its unique juxtaposition of dust and color, abject poverty and profound spirituality.

The big, old car took us as close to the New Diamond Hotel as was physically possible and we walked the last 50 yards jumping over puddles and dodging the filth and feces littering the pathway. Bhote Bahal was one of the poorer parts of the city, located a short walk from the bottom end of Freak Street, named for the hippy clientele of the 60s and 70s.

Though the staff remembered us and welcomed us like long lost friends, I could tell that Rosemarie and Carl were less than comfortable with their temporary lodgings. Stoically, they agreed to the 40-rupee tariff (less than $1), and we were led to our separate rooms on the rooftop level. I think it was the state of the shared bathroom that sealed their decision to move on the next day. That, and the more attractive and appropriately named Earth House, which they had found nestled in the heart of Thamel, the new tourist haunt.

We met them for breakfast a couple of days after their move, in a restaurant at the bottom of Freak Street that had become our local. It had a menu that was four pages long. They marveled over the extensive list of offerings, from muesli and yoghurt to laksa and Asian dumplings. They even had Vegemite toast. They were very happy in their new hotel room and implored us to also move 'toward the Earth.' Reluctantly, we agreed.

It was indeed a much more inviting, and cleaner, place than the New Diamond, which paled in comparison. Surrounded by a high wall that enclosed well-tended gardens, it had a charm and character in keeping with its name. The upstairs rooms boasted traditional, carved wooden windows that looked out over a courtyard decorated with cane furniture covered in colorful cushions. But the trade-off was the noise from the local traffic. Car horns, bicycle bells, and shouting voices floated over the whitewashed walls without hindrance.

During our two-year absence, Thamel had become the new tourist hotspot. A plethora of restaurants and cafes served fair renditions of dishes from around the world. Some of the shops in the area even had real glass windows. Our love of coffee and cake drew us into a tiny hole-in-the-wall café just off the main square. It wasn't much to look at. There was no ambience to speak of, but a friendly and softly spoken young man worked there, and he welcomed us with a huge smile whenever we stopped by. He didn't bake the amazing array of cakes that adorned the shelves in the front window, but he served them well and made a decent cup of joe.

After many mid-morning visits, we grew to like him a lot and our conversations over cake became a highlight of our day. We enjoyed his good-natured company, asking his advice about all things Nepali and answering his many questions about our lives in Japan. It was a friendship that would grow to have great meaning for us all in the years to come.

The immigration office had also moved into a building just off the main square, creating even more traffic and chaos. Everyday hundreds of foreigners lounged around the square, reading, chatting, and whiling away time waiting for visas and permits. Noisy rickshaws plied the streets looking for fares. It was constantly bustling.

We too made use of our proximity to these offices to secure permits for the Annapurna Sanctuary trek, but we only lasted a couple of days at the Earth House before returning to the relative peace and paucity on the opposite side of town. Then we began to prepare to leave the valley and head over to Pokhara in western Nepal.

29

POKHARA AND THE SANCTUARY

*L*ocated on the shores of scenic Phewa Tal, the tourist strip in Pokhara was just a rough, dirt road along the edge of the lake, lined with cheap backpacker hotels and cafes. Since our last visit to western Nepal, a lot more trekking agencies had sprung up, presumably to service the increasing number of organized groups frequenting the Himalayan trails. But apart from that, it hadn't changed much; the atmosphere was still laid-back Bohemian. Its obvious popularity loudly proclaimed that it was still a great place to relax, veg out, and prepare for a trek in the Annapurna. Or recover from one.

On our initial trek in the Himalaya, we had also set out from Pokhara almost five years before. We had walked out of town one fine morning, climbed our first decent hill, and promptly offloaded our sleeping bags with the first farmhouse family that offered us a cup of *chia*.[1] Now there was a road that took prospective trekkers into the foothills, eliminating at least two days' walk. The road was rough, but the reconfigured jeeps covered the distance and crawled up the hills faster than we could walk. So, we joined the crowd waiting at the appointed departure point, purchased our tickets, and climbed aboard.

But this time, instead of making our way toward the pilgrimage site of Muktinath, where most of our fellow trekkers were headed, we opted for the fork in the trail at the village of Birethanti that would lead us into the Annapurna Sanctuary.

Mani was almost four years old when we embarked on this trek; too heavy to carry and too young to cover the distances required to make it from village to village as per the usual route. So, our pace was slowed to match his. This was a good thing. We walked with different people each day rather than meeting the same group of faces in the lodges every evening. We were always a day or two behind. It was Mani who made new friends, and we were simply caught up in the introductions and interactions that he initiated. If not for his gregarious nature, it would have been a much lonelier trek for James and me.

At the bottom of one of the biggest hills of the trek, a three-hour uphill climb to the village of Ghandruk, we stopped for lunch. Mani wasn't hungry, only thirsty, and not feeling a hundred percent. We made him eat some plain rice, which he washed down with a bottle of Fanta (his choice) and promptly vomited up. He didn't want to go any further, especially not uphill. So, there was nothing for it. James took the second backpack, wearing the two of them like a sandwich board, and I carried Mani on my back. For three hours. When we reached the village of Ghandruk, we were both utterly spent.

Ghandruk was perched on the side of a heavily terraced mountain that reached up into the sky in one direction and down into a deep valley in the other. Its slate laneways were lined by buildings with ochre-washed walls, and as we entered, it began to rain. We chose the first lodge we came across as our shelter for the night. A young lad in dirty white pants and long kurta shirt led us up to a room on the second floor. Its wooden-shuttered windows looked out towards the mountain on the opposite side of the valley, and as I sat at the tiny desk writing in my journal, mist rolled in and covered the village so that we appeared to be floating amongst the clouds. It was magical.

We all slept well that night and when we woke the next morning, the sun was shining, the mountains were clear, and Mani, obviously feeling better, was demanding breakfast. Everything was as it should be again. Today's destination was Chomrong, the last permanent settlement outside the Sanctuary.

It should have been a five-hour walk, but with one reasonable climb and one steep climb, coupled with our snail's pace, it took all day. Rain decided to return about an hour before we reached Chomrong, making the trail very slippery. So, once again, we arrived exhausted and sodden, our clothes plastered to our skin. The rain also didn't bode well for the next day's walk. Rain at this altitude equaled snow up higher, and snow could make the trails impassable and close the Sanctuary.

We spent the night in Chomrong in a fantastic, warm lodge that would have afforded a magnificent view of the Annapurna range had it not been for the rain. Mani introduced us to his new friends Chuck and Ramsay from the States, who appeared to have as much fun as he did as they tossed a ball around the huge dirt forecourt of the lodge.

In the morning, we awoke to the bad news that there had been a serious avalanche not too far up the trail and the path into the Sanctuary was cut. Rumor had it that a couple of trekkers had died. We weren't going any further. The decision to return to Pokhara was made for us.

It took several more days to return to the relative warmth and humidity of the lakeside village with its comfy hotels and amazing food. We delayed our boneshaking bus trip back to Kathmandu for as long as we could, but Japan and the jobs to which we must return loomed large in the back of our minds. Our love for Nepal had grown with every visit we made to the kingdom. We had real friends in Kathmandu, friends that had supported us in the learning journey that was our travel lives. They greeted us warmly every time we returned, and we looked forward to catching up with them again and again.

But eventually, we just had to drag ourselves away.

∽

30

BEDSIDE MANNER

We hadn't been back from Nepal long when I fell pregnant with our second child. I was never one to visit a doctor unnecessarily, so it wasn't unusual that I didn't have a designated GP. I had only seen a doctor once in the first six months of my first pregnancy, and that was in Kathmandu.

The antique American medic who owned the uptown Roppongi practice had an ultrasound machine in his consulting room, something I'd only previously experienced in a dedicated clinic. I guess that's why it cost $100 USD to see him for 15 minutes. He used it on me immediately and confirmed that I was indeed pregnant. *Great, we established that which I already knew.* He went on to say that while there was what he called a fetal area on the ultrasound picture, there didn't appear to be an actual fetus. But it was early days, just a few weeks by my calculation, so we both assumed it was just too soon to have something more concrete to look at. We decided on a wait and watch approach.

I discovered the inhumanity of the Japanese doctor's office the hard way, when this unplanned pregnancy ended abruptly at four and a half months. A miscarriage is never an easy thing to go through, but it's just that bit harder when you're living in a foreign country, far from home and people who can support you in your own language. But life happens no matter where you are; you have to deal with it.

It happened one Sunday night a few months later, at about 9 p.m. The waiting part was suddenly over.

"I think I need to go to a hospital." I was standing in the kitchen holding my stomach, wincing with the pain of almost continuous contractions, and bleeding all over the floor.

"What? Why?" James looked up from his book and stared at me, his brow furrowed with concern. He had no idea what was happening, or why I'd spent the last hour in the bathroom.

"Something's wrong. I think I might be having a miscarriage." Total understatement. It could hardly have been more definite. "Maybe we should call a taxi." I could scarcely believe what I was suggesting, my one and only taxi experience being the day we moved into the house.

I guess it sounded a bit odd, too. Why would you call a taxi instead of an ambulance? But here's the thing. We didn't own a vehicle at the time, and neither did any of our friends who lived close by. Because I knew how expensive everything was in Japan, I assumed that calling an ambulance without having insurance would be unaffordable, just like at home. But if we did call a taxi, where on earth would we ask him to go? There were no hospitals close by. At least, I hadn't seen any on my bicycle rides around the neighborhood. It started to get a bit scary. This wasn't something I'd planned for, and I suddenly felt very vulnerable. I couldn't think clearly and deal with the cramps and an urge to push at the same time. I rushed back to the bathroom.

We decided to phone Molly, our friend who lived around the corner, and ask her advice. She had a young baby and might actually know where we should go. As luck would have it, she had a Japanese friend visiting that night. She put Kyoko on the phone, and she immediately suggested we call an ambulance.

"I don't think we can afford it, Kyoko. We don't have any insurance."

"But the ambulance service is free in Japan. And they will know where to take you. A taxi driver will just be angry. I will call one for you. What is your address?" I was stunned beyond belief, and a little bit relieved. I had no desire to do battle with a disgruntled Tokyo taxi driver again, especially when it was certain I was going to bleed all over his white lace seat covers on the way to wherever we had to go.

The ambulance arrived promptly, lights and sirens at full throttle. Kyoko and Molly followed the medics in the door, which was fortunate. Kyoko was able to explain to the attendants exactly what had happened and translate their questions for me. Medical terminology had not been high on my 'vocab I should learn first up' list. As they carried me out on a stretcher, I imagined our landlady and her husband peering through the upstairs windows that overlooked our house wondering what on earth the crazy *gaijin* next door were up to now.

The ride to the nearest hospital that was open at that time of night took about 30 minutes, and James, Mani and I traveled all the way with the lights flashing and the siren blaring, despite my pleas that it was unnecessary. It was clearly upsetting my four-year-old son, who clutched his teddy as if his life depended on it. I don't think they understood me, though. The medic just patted my arm and smiled benevolently.

I was in and out of surgery in what seemed like an instant but must have actually taken about an hour. I came around from the anesthetic to find a doctor standing at the end of my bed studying a file and looking nervous and worried. A white surgical mask dangled from one ear. He wiped his hand across his mouth and frowned. He didn't seem to know what to say.

"No baby!" he blurted, almost exhausting the limits of his knowledge of English with those two words.

"What? What are you talking about? How could there possibly be no baby when I've just undergone surgery for a miscarriage? It doesn't make any sense." I couldn't lift my head from the pillow let alone fathom what on earth he meant.

"No baby!" He just kept repeating himself. It was extraordinary, and unsettling. A nurse entered the room, also wearing a white mask.

"We didn't find any baby," she chimed in, as if that explained the situation better. "Maybe baby at home?"

Well, there had been a lot of blood at home, but I was pretty certain that I had not delivered a baby in the toilet, and I definitely hadn't been rushed to the hospital in the middle of the night while the said baby was left at home. They didn't believe me.

"No baby here. Someone must bring baby." I almost laughed, but judging by the look on their faces, that was really the wrong response. It couldn't have been more ludicrous. And they seemed determined to keep me in the hospital until I produced the missing baby.

It must have been the leftover anesthetic that made me bold, and I tried to explain in a mixture of English and bad Japanese that I wasn't hiding the baby at home, but that I needed to go home as soon as possible. In the end, I gave up and delivered my soliloquy in English.

"I can't stay in the hospital for even one day. I have a toddler to look after. My husband has a job. He can't get time off at the drop of a hat, and there is no one else who can help. My family is 5,000 miles and more than 24 hours away even if they get straight on a plane. That isn't going to happen. They don't even know I'm pregnant. I have to go home. And soon."

They were unmoved. More likely, they hadn't understood a word I said. The wheels on my bed were unlocked and I was trundled off to a room somewhere upstairs. When I asked where James and Mani were, I was told they had left. This was more distressing than the miscarriage at that point. It wasn't until the next morning that I learnt they had been sent home to 'look for the baby.'

I was awakened very early by a disembodied voice, addressing me in Japanese. It was only just light, but I could see that there was no one in the room apart from me. I looked around, alarmed, and discovered that the female voice was coming from a speaker mounted in the ceiling of the room. I had no idea what was being said or asked. All I managed to catch was the word *asagohan*.[1]

"*Wakarimasen*,"[2] I said to no one in particular, and felt rather stupid speaking to an empty room. "I don't understand." It was all I could manage.

Shortly after the announcement, a nurse entered and presented me with a breakfast tray: green tea, rice, a piece of fish, some pickles, and a raw egg. A traditional Japanese breakfast. Perhaps that was what I was being asked. Or more likely told. "Breakfast will be served." I'm not fond of raw eggs. And I hate fish. I pushed the tray aside, taking only the tea.

"Where is my husband? *Shujin*? Has he come back yet? When can I leave? I have to go home today. I can't stay here." She smiled weakly and bowed ever so slightly without saying a word. It was more of a nod than a bow. It wasn't even close to a yes. But it wasn't a no either. "Doctor come. Speak." She left the room.

It was a good hour before doctor-come-speak appeared in my room. It wasn't the same one who had attended me the night before.

"I am Dr. Takano. This is my clinic. We did not find any baby. We must investigate. You may return home today if everything is okay. But you must return here in three days. Please make appointment time before you leave."

"What do you mean investigate? Why was there no baby?"

"We are not sure. We will do blood test." His manner was serious. He wasn't used to being quizzed. He was the *sensei*[3] and the only appropriate response to such a superior being was "*Hai, sensei*. Thank you."

"Can I go right now?"

"Hmm… " He hesitated, searching for the right words. "When your… your husband come. Please wait here." With that he left the room. A middle-aged nurse in an impossibly starched, pale green uniform, armed with a tray full of vials, needles, and various other instruments necessary for obtaining blood, bowed as she entered my room. She didn't say a word, but it was obvious what was going to happen next. Blood was taken with practiced ease. Lots and lots of blood.

Rather than wait around for James and Mani to come and find me, which may not have been easy, I got dressed and made my way to the nurses' station halfway down the corridor. I was lightheaded, probably from the amount of blood that had been extracted, not to mention what I had lost during the whole ordeal. I wasn't aware of the full impact of what I was doing, but no one tried to stop me. They probably weren't used to disobedient patients.

The building was quite small, not like a hospital at all, except that there were lots of women in pale green uniforms wearing white masks at every turn. They whispered to each other as I passed and pointed in the direction of an elevator. I was on the third floor of a building no bigger than a small block of apartments.

Even though it was only 7 a.m., the reception area was full of waiting patients, young and old, all wearing white masks. It reminded me of a scene from a war zone. They all turned and stared at the *gaijin* in their midst, then quickly averted their gaze. I was suddenly acutely aware that I must have looked like a train wreck. I should have waited for James to come with fresh clothes. The ones I had come in with were crumpled and mismatched. I also had no shoes, only the plastic hospital slippers that had been provided in my room. I decided to take a seat and wait for inspiration.

I wondered what kind of clinic this was. I also wondered where it was, since I had no idea where the ambulance had taken me last night. A woman behind the reception desk beckoned to me and handed me a piece of paper on which was written a date and time. She probably explained that it was my next appointment, so I nodded and said, "*Hai, hai.*" When in doubt, just agree. It could all be figured out later. I just wanted to go home.

There was a public phone in the waiting room, but I had no money to call home to find out when James and Mani would be back. And there were no mobile phones in 1987. I had no choice but to sit and wait for them. It was a long uncomfortable, two-hour wait in dirty, scruffy clothes. When they eventually arrived, we had to walk over a mile to the nearest train station, catch a train to Matsudo, take a bus from Matsudo station, and then walk down the hill to our home. Looking back now, it seems ludicrous that we didn't just take a taxi. But at the time, that's the way it went. Plus, I hated taxis.

31

NO BABY

I returned to the clinic three days later at the appointed time, not quite sure what to expect. The receptionist motioned for me to sit. Obediently, I did as I was instructed. Sometimes I felt that living in Japan was turning me back into a sheep, a follower of rules, many of which I didn't agree with. But rocking the boat was not the Japanese way. And it was definitely not the way to get things done. The rules would be followed, *gaijin* or no.

After a masked nurse called my name, I was led down a corridor and into another large room that contained a long desk, divided into four sections by three vertical panels. At each cubicle, a man in a white coat sat talking to other patients. Facing them, on a bench seat that lined the opposite wall, were another three patients whom I recognized from the waiting room outside. I took my seat, and we all pretended not to listen to the medical problems being discussed with the doctors. For my part it didn't matter. I couldn't understand a word of what was being said. But for everyone else there was a complete lack of privacy.

When my turn came around, I sat before an older gentleman, the one who had introduced himself to me as the owner of the clinic in the room upstairs several days ago.

"*Chotto matte kudasai.*"[1] He stood and walked to a large bookshelf at the back of the room. When he returned, he placed a bulky textbook in front of me, open at a page entitled Hydatidiform Mole. It was entirely in English.

"Please read. I will make a copy for you."

As my eyes skimmed over the article, I realized this was his way of telling me what had happened to me. The next words out of his mouth were scary.

"Possible cancer. Very bad one." There's a lot to be said for the subtleties of nuance when delivered in your native tongue. This diagnosis was given in blunt, one-syllable blows, each one an apparent death sentence.

I looked up, not quite getting it, not wanting to. There was a lot to take in. I glanced behind me to see who else was overhearing this dreadful diagnosis. Of course, all heads were bowed, and no one seemed to be paying attention.

"You can read later. I will see you every month for the next two years. Bring sample every month." He pushed a small, plastic container with a bright yellow lid towards me. "Do not have a baby! You understand? No baby!" Those words again. No baby. Only this time, it was a directive, not an observation. He held my gaze. It was unusual for a Japanese person to maintain eye contact for so long.

"Why was there no baby?" I asked him. In answer, he stabbed his finger at the article.

"You can read here." It was as much as I was going to get. The language barrier was too great for this kind of explanation. "Come back in one month. Please bring with you." He motioned towards the container. And with that I was dismissed.

So, that's how it went for the next two years, monthly visits where my urine was tested for the offending hormones that would indicate whether cancer was developing. It became routine and uneventful, apart from the second, post-operative visit.

I was ushered into the interior waiting area as usual, except this time I was instructed to enter one of the curtained cubicles to the right of the consulting desks. I was invited to disrobe from the waist down and lay on the examination table with a sheet covering the lower half of my body. I noticed with some trepidation that if I did so, a curtain would bisect my supine form so that I could no longer see what was going on on the other side of it.

Obediently, I lay there wondering what horrendous fate awaited me. It wasn't hard to work out and I didn't have long to mull it over. There was a bit of a commotion on the other side of the curtain, and without warning, a faceless, silent someone conducted an internal examination. I never saw the face of my violator, nor heard his voice. He spoke only one word when he was done. "Okay."

At first, I was just shocked, but when the repulsion of what had just happened set in, I felt assaulted. On a purely academic level, I understood that the intention of the anonymity was to save me the embarrassment of watching someone carry out the examination. But it had the reverse effect of feeling more like a rape. Far from protecting me from embarrassment, I was humiliated, reduced to a nameless, faceless body part to be examined and assessed in the name of medical science. It was an ordeal I wished never to repeat, and has no doubt contributed to my lifelong distrust of the medical profession.

After that trauma, I'm not sure where I found the courage to return every month for the next two years. Perhaps it was the sense of impending doom that had been instilled in me at the first postnatal visit. Perhaps I had been brainwashed by a society that seemed destined to bow, obey, and be grateful for any attention from those perceived to be in positions of power. It certainly wasn't a kind and gentle bedside manner that kept me going back but go back I did. And I made sure I didn't fall pregnant again within the designated time. Two years. No way I was going through this experience again. Not in Japan. Maybe not ever.

JOURNAL

July 10

We lost the baby last Sunday night. I'd had some contractions on Friday, which came to nothing. But they started up again on Sunday evening and it wasn't too long before it all went pear-shaped. It happened quickly and I'm glad it happened at home. In that way there really was a birth and we were all a part of it.

Once inside the hospital I was cut off from James and Mani, and even from my own body by curtains, drips, blindfolds, and anesthetic. Yes, a blindfold was placed over my eyes for some unknown reason. It was the stuff of nightmares, but I managed to convince them that they were overcompensating. They removed the blindfold and finally agreed to let me go home the next day if I was okay. I was. It's not an experience I hope to ever repeat. I had to go back yesterday for a checkup, and I was told I could stop taking the medication and resume normal activities. The doctor seemed quite amazed at my recovery. I guess I should have told him I hadn't taken his wretched pills as he probably thought they had done their job very efficiently.

Anyways, I feel okay physically, feeding myself garlic oil and living on a diet of fruit for a good detox. I don't feel so sad about the baby leaving us; these things happen, conditions were just not right. I got the distinct feeling that *the doctors and nurses at the clinic were trying to pretend nothing had happened. Perhaps they were trying to protect me in their own weird way. The blindfold didn't help in that regard. It was quite unsettling.*

Although it isn't something I feel I can discuss at length with anyone, I still need to get out a lot of the feelings about the miscarriage that have gone unsaid. I do feel angry and upset, though not with anyone or anything in particular. Except perhaps the universe.

It helps to write about it. Some experiences are very difficult to share with those who haven't had a similar experience. So, we share those experiences with people whom we think will understand, not just because they've been there, but because they want to be there.

Since James and I began traveling, we've had to learn how to cope with the ups and downs of life alone and together. And that includes ups and downs in our health. It's made us vulnerable, but it's also made us stronger in lots of ways, given us back some of the power to heal ourselves that social institutions would so swiftly take away.

Yet somehow, this shared belief and common experience between James and I doesn't make difficult conversations any easier. We haven't really talked about the physical or emotional impact of losing a baby. Some people never get over it. Some poor souls go through it over and over again. How unfair is that? I feel resigned to the fact that it's happened; surprised, I guess, but I'm still largely dealing with it alone. I don't have any idea how James feels about it. We talk without really talking. We go through the motions day by day. Somehow, we are able to have deep and meaningful discussions about anything but our own emotions. We have slipped into a relationship more akin to best friends or brother and sister than lifelong partners. Sadly, we have come to share a distance that is becoming increasingly difficult to bridge.

33

LEARNING NIHONGO

*A*fter losing the baby, I needed a project to throw myself into. Perhaps it was time to formalize my study of the Japanese language. It was certainly a useful tool to have in the kit. I was proud of the way I had managed so far: renting the house, conversing with the supermarket cashiers, asking for directions, and navigating the rail system. But an interesting, extended conversation on a current affairs topic, or deciphering the hieroglyphics that was the Japanese writing system? Not so good.

The Japanese written word was complicated. There were three ways to write; *kanji* had been lifted directly from Chinese because Japan didn't actually have a written language back in the day. The trouble was, it didn't quite work for them and needed to be adapted to fit. Hence the invention of *hiragana*, the Japanese alphabet, and *katakana*, a phonetic rendition of the English alphabet. To make matters worse, the 2,000 most frequently used *kanji* characters consisted of anywhere from one to twenty-four different pen strokes. And you needed to memorize at least 1500 characters if you hoped to ever read a newspaper or magazine. Students graduated high school able to read at least that many, often more.

The most basic *kanji* were originally derived from pictures of what was seen. For example, the character for water developed from squeezing the middle of the character for river. Squeeze a river and what do you get? Water. Each word was usually composed of two *kanji* and there were several elements contained within each character. Another example, the character for every was composed of the characters for man and mother — because every man has a mother. The character for east was comprised of the ones that represented the sun and a tree. The sun rises up behind the tree — in the east.

One of the guys from the *gaijin* house had pointed out to me that the character for prostitute contained three parts: woman, sell, and spring. Hence the character translated from 'a woman selling spring' — somewhat euphemistic, and not one I would ever get to use, but he possibly already had.

So, I set about looking for a teacher with whom I could get a more formal grounding in the language than I was getting from my *Let's Learn Japanese* phrasebook and dictionary.

Enter Noguchi-san. We met once a week in a coffee shop in Ichikawa, *sans* Mani, and for about an hour and ¥1,000 she guided me through the language course and answered my constant questions. After a few months, we even started to have discussions that didn't spring from textbook prompts and more reasonably reflected subjects I was interested in. It was always difficult to get her opinion, or that of any Japanese person to be honest. They didn't want to discuss politics, morality, or religion lest someone be offended. Sheesh!

One day, I asked her to teach me the word for fuck, as in, "What the fuck?"

"Come on," I pleaded. "There must be a word you use when things go wrong." It didn't help that Japanese has different vocabulary and speech patterns depending on the gender of the speaker, and while the male version of the language was much more colorful, women just shouldn't be heard to utter such words. Finally, she admitted there was something I could say, but reiterated that I should never say it.

"Ma," she whispered, looking furtively around the cafe to ensure she had not been heard.

"Ma?" I exploded at the top of my voice. "Ma? That's it? Ma?" Noguchi-san was literally hiding under the table as the word reverberated off the walls and all heads turned our way.

"Shhhhh! Shhhhh! Don't say it!" She was so embarrassed and all I could do was laugh. It seemed too mild and inadequate to replace its expressive English counterpart.

The two distinct levels of speech for men and women got the girls who worked in the hostess bars into trouble on many occasions. Spending their evenings lighting cigarettes and pouring drinks in bars exclusively frequented by men, they picked up the basest level of the language, causing one of my students to comment, "She speaks like truck driver." There was also another level, the honorific form that was used in formal conversation with superiors, elders, mentors, or teachers. It was a minefield, bound to trip up even the most earnest student of the language.

Eventually, I reached a point where I could ask just about any question. The problem lay with the answer. I couldn't catch it. So, to save face, I pretended.

"*Hai, hai, hai,*" I would say, bowing as I went on my merry way with no clue as to the answer. Occasionally, the answer would come to me later as a complete sentence that I fully understood. Unfortunately, it was too late by then to be of any use to me.

Before we left the country, and with Noguchi-san's ever so patient dedication to the cause, I sat the Japanese Language Proficiency Examination at a level which required a working knowledge of about 1,000 *kanji* characters. And passed. It was a gratifying achievement, one that capped a very long and inelegant learning curve.

Though I have little cause to speak or read Japanese these days, I do sometimes hold little practice conversations in my head. I never cease to amaze myself at some of the random vocabulary I manage to dredge up. It must be a bit like riding a bike. Once you know how, it's in there forever — somewhere.

34

HOMESCHOOL JOURNEY

*1*988 was the year Mani turned four and we started to think about our options for his education. Right from the start of our deliberations, putting him into the Japanese education system was out of the question. Its regimented, one size fits all approach to learning just didn't gel with our lifestyle or our philosophy. We had been profoundly influenced by the writings of an American psychologist, Dr. Joseph Chilton Pearce, and his work on child development. After reading his books and attending one of his lectures when he visited Tokyo, the Japanese school system was right off the table. There was no way we were ever going to subject our child to such a rigid and inflexible education. We wanted Mani to experience the world from a hands-on perspective. That's why we'd spent the early years of his life ferrying him around the world with us wherever we went. We worked off the premise that if children weren't welcome, we weren't welcome either. And we avoided that place, function, or event.

During the early days in the *gaijin* house, Mani had spent almost all his time in the company of adults. He was extremely active and endlessly curious, and we had encouraged him to explore everything without fear. But he still needed to learn some of the more traditional subjects, and the only other option was to teach him ourselves. We were going to have to home school.

Putting together a homeschooling curriculum in a non-English speaking country was not only challenging, it was downright impossible to do with only local resources. Homeschooling was unheard of in Japan, and still in its infancy in both Australia and the USA. Many of those taking on the challenge were doing so for religious reasons. Others, like us, were just disillusioned with the system. Somehow, we managed to track down companies in the States that were putting together educational toys and tools that supported our endeavors, and we became their biggest fans. We found a handful of educational materials in various disciplines that could keep our young Einstein engaged. He didn't care much for math; in fact, it often sent him into a meltdown. But science, art, geography, and a mountain of Lego bricks could keep him enthralled for hours.

Computers were still largely unavailable in the late 1980s. Apple had recently released their IIe model and were about to go to market with one of the first portable computers, the PowerBook. But with a price tag of around ¥350,000 for a bare bones model, they were beyond our reach. They were also cumbersome and not particularly user friendly. And the Internet, well that was still a dream. I read that some guy who worked for the US Department of Defense had developed it about 20 years before, but no one really knew about it. For me, though, I yearned for a way to network with other homeschooling families. I didn't know what it was called back then, but I understood how truly useful it was going to be.

Because there was no Internet, finding resources was all about libraries. The excellent World Magazine Gallery in the Ginza helped us narrow our search. We became catalogue junkies, ordering curricula, books, and supplies from those we sourced in various alternative magazines such as *Utne Reader* and *Mother Jones*. A magazine called *Growing Without Schooling* quickly became the staple in our constant search for new ideas and teaching materials.

We had so much fun, I'm not sure who enjoyed our purchases more, Mani or us. We couldn't wait for the postman to deliver our latest spoils, and when a parcel arrived, we tore into it and spent hours listening to professionally recorded cassettes of stories set to music, challenging our math skills with new tricks and shortcuts, creating mind-blowing science experiments, and putting together model toys. Hours of fun and excitement, all in the spirit of learning. And Mani loved it.

He particularly loved his stories but preferred to have them told to him rather than read for himself. To create some free time for myself, and to avoid reading the same tales over and over again, I invested a great deal of time late at night, after he had finally gone to bed, recording them onto a stack of cassette tapes. He listened so often he wore them out. On more than one occasion, I would begin the first paragraph only to have him recite the next few from memory. Together we worked our way through the entire C. S. Lewis *Narnia* series, Arthur Ransome's *Swallows and Amazons*, all the *Tin Tin* comics, the complete children's works of Roald Dahl, Kenneth Grahame's *Wind in the Willows*. The list went on and on.

It wasn't all plain sailing though. Science was also a favorite. And art. Even social studies. He knew the globe by heart and could name capital cities as well as countries. But everything came to a sudden stop when it wasn't perceived as fun. Setting a time limit to complete various math tasks would send him into a spin, even though I knew he was up for the challenge. Adding the element of competition, even against himself, was too much and often ended in tears — sometimes mine for even suggesting it in the first place. Because there was so much else going on, I took the easy option and let it ride. Anything for peace.

James didn't want me to work when we moved to Japan. He wanted me to stay at home and be a full-time mum. Before we began traveling, I had always worked, and had always enjoyed my work, not so much for the tasks as the camaraderie and social life that went with it. So, I was a little taken aback by the prospect of being confined to quarters, and initially at least, took some convincing. His income alone was certainly enough to support us, but not working eroded my sense of independence. I was torn between wanting a job and an income of my own and wanting to be with my son. I cherished the time I spent with Mani, but I suffered from a lack of adult interaction at the same time.

I believe that lack of interaction contributed to my susceptibility to control. I was isolated, with only James for company and community, and he had a happy knack of making me feel guilty about my choices. Even in the supermarket, if he was shopping with me, I bought the things that he approved of rather than the things I preferred, like white rice instead of brown. It wasn't something that happened overnight. There were years between the once strong-minded mother figure I imagined myself to be and the acquiescent shadow I would become. Slowly but surely, I adopted the mantle of obedience of my childhood days.

Because I had always worked, it was hard not to now. But instead of making a stand for my financial and emotional independence, I submitted. At the time, I probably told myself it was the right thing to do; I certainly wasn't the first or only woman to give up work for the care of their family. But in the back of my mind, I felt like I had given up something important to me. I buried that feeling deep under the busy-ness of our new life in this foreign country: organizing, caring, shopping, cooking, homemaking. But the fact remained that I had taken someone else's opinion as my own, bowed to someone else's will, given away a little bit of my power. And so, perhaps unwittingly at first, it gradually became a pattern in our marriage, supported by the larger Japanese psychosocial order.

Looking back now, I wonder whether seemingly insignificant decisions often lead to more toxic relationships, whether simple benign acquiescence contributes to submission on deeper levels. Perhaps a lack of opposition is easily mistaken for agreement, and eventually leads to the loss of greater liberties.

It stood to reason that if I couldn't get out of the house to earn money, then I should try to earn the money by working from home. So, I agreed to take on the babysitting of Molly's baby daughter. I had planned to try to earn some money from my writing, but with this new gig the barriers to writing just multiplied. She seemed much more of a handful than I remembered Mani ever being, and I often found it difficult to get her settled. Maybe it was partly my attitude; I never saw myself as a babysitter. My own child had never been away from me and here I was looking after someone else's on a semi-permanent basis. My afternoons and evenings devolved into a humdrum childcare routine and my writing and Mani's homeschooling flew quietly out the window, along with any further opportunity to work.

Living in Japan put us in an awkward no man's land of cultural incongruence. All of a sudden, we were *gaijin*, part of a group that by its very nomenclature meant outsider, as well as foreigner. Though we may have appeared to adapt and fit in with various local customs, we would never be seen as Japanese, relegated always to the outside looking in. Yet by our own choice, we were also isolated from the outsider's community. Perhaps it was misguided, but we spent little time outside of work with any other foreigners, preferring to immerse ourselves in a society that would never fully accept us.

35
JOURNAL

September 16

There just aren't enough hours in the day anymore. Write letters, read books, study Japanese, meet James for lunch in Matsudo, take Mani to the park, babysit friend's child, try to do some writing, meditate, read more books, deal with the idiosyncrasies of life in Japan. There's always something to be done, and Mani ensures I do each thing for no longer than five minutes at a time. "Can you get me something to eat? To drink? Where's this? Where's that? Can we go to a park? Come and watch me cook dinner/ride my bike!" And I'm thinking of adding a correspondence course in homeopathy into the mix. But where will I squeeze it in? Somewhere between cooking, shopping, and cleaning up, I guess.

Having become involved in homeschooling, I have realized it is not such an unusual thing to do, especially in the States. Many families have made the decision to either take their kids out of school or not send them at all. It's a decision of responsibility really and I admit it's not a light one. Teaching your own child gives you freedom to present the world from any and many points of view, not in one rigid way geared to answering questions in some irrelevant test paper. We all know an arts degree is not worth the paper it's written on these days and having one only opens certain doors. Many tertiary *institutions now recognize the validity of life experience in educational evaluation procedures and are prepared to give credit for that towards a degree or even a masters. Just because learning does not take place within an institution does not reduce its validity.*

One thing an institution does do, and does very well, is take away the knowledge that we have a choice. People amaze me when they say they envy our lifestyle – living here and there, traveling around, free to do anything (yes, some people say that); then they add a list of reasons why they can't do the same thing: a house, mortgage payments, a car, family, job. They see all those things as security, and they choose to have them. You can choose not to, but it doesn't lessen either your responsibility or security. In fact, the result is just the opposite. Freedom is actually more responsibility and more security in yourself. The paradox is, you can't see that from the pre-choice side. It's a leap of faith in truth, nature, God, yourself, whatever you want to call it. Some people are not ready to accept that, and that's a choice too. We all have to live with our own choices. Other people can guide us with their experiences, but they cannot live our lives for us, as much as they may want to.

My Japanese has reached the stage where I can say many things and be reasonably sure of being understood — ask directions, ask about the food or whatever I'm buying. But I still have trouble understanding the answers. I get words here and there that enable me to piece together an appropriate response, or at least a simplified question of their statement. But no matter how much I learn, it's never enough to be fluent. Some people are easier to understand than others, but some gobble up what words I might possibly understand by covering their mouths with their hands, a habit I loathe. They may as well be speaking in tongues.

The weather is really fouled up at the moment, with the emphasis on foul. We had practically no summer, the rainy season lasted two months instead of one and nearly ruined the rice crop, and yesterday a typhoon blew through Tokyo leaving a big freeze in its wake. We were out in sweaters yesterday, and today has been the hottest September day on record. And it's raining again. The typhoon took all the smog away. We could do with one every day on that score. Today the sky and the river both look blue.

Disneyland's evening fireworks display is going off just now, clear as a bell. Most nights we can barely see them. Matsudo didn't have its fireworks display this year because the river has been in flood for the last month. They're usually held on the riverbanks all around the country and Matsudo has one of the largest displays in Tokyo, taking one and a half hours to let off about 13,000 fireworks. Now I know where our taxes go, though we don't pay much compared to back home. Personal income tax is pretty low at around seven percent.

I'm still going to the doctor about once a month because nobody can seem to agree on how long follow-up should be for this postnatal condition. Every time I go, I see someone different. It seems you don't really have a doctor in Japan; you belong to the institution.

As of next week, I'm an English teacher again. A lady approached me in the park and asked me to teach her kids and her friends' kids twice a month. It turns out the kids are one and a half, two, three, and five, and there's about nine of them. Why do I agree to these things? I think she only wants me to play with them for about half an hour, then spend an hour and a half in informal conversation with the mothers while the kids entertain themselves under the watchful eye of the lady's mother. There are four women and I've met three of them. Two are not afraid to speak English despite the mistakes they make, which is quite rare because the Japanese aren't usually willing to make public mistakes. Mani had a wonderful time with them all last week when we went to meet the crowd and make the arrangements. They have so many toys.

~

1989

36
DEGREE, VISA, JOB — CHECK

Staying home with Mani kept me more than busy. We had gotten into a routine of fixing lunch for James and riding up to Matsudo to share it with him during his break late in the afternoon. When I failed to find the time to make lunch because Mani and I were reading together or out on the bike shopping or exploring the area, we'd go to have lunch with James anyway, grabbing ourselves some sushi at the takeaway located in the Box Hill department store. I was particularly fond of the long rolls of *ume-shiso* and *natto*. Box Hill was also home to one of the most delicious bakeries this side of the Edo River. They made a phenomenal pumpkin and walnut pie wrapped in puff pastry, and delightful little rolls filled with cheese and mayonnaise. Reluctantly, I had to give these up when we decided to become vegan, but there were plenty of goodies to fill the gap. It was easy to be vegan in Japan because of the abundance of delicious soy products. It was just as well we rode our bikes everywhere to work off all the calories.

James had longed to swap places with me for some time. Though he quite enjoyed the work he was doing, he felt he was missing out on Mani growing up. By the time he got home from Berlitz at around 9:30 p.m. he was dog-tired. Mani, on the other hand, was not, and usually stayed awake in full flight until past 11 p.m. One night, James voiced the opinion that maybe I should take on some of the financial responsibility so that he could take his turn at staying home with Mani.

It didn't seem an unreasonable ask. I was doing what I could, and I admit that most of the motivation for taking on classes with little kids was more for Mani's benefit than mine. Dancing around like a clown, entertaining Japanese tiny tots may have been one way to boost our household budget, but the time spent in such frivolous activities far outweighed any fiscal advantage gained. And patching together a few more formal classes with eager businessmen and housewives wasn't going to cut it either. It had become apparent that the longer we stayed in Tokyo, the more money we needed. Our savings were still mounting up, but our desire to do more than just eat, sleep, and work had also grown. We were living in one of the most interesting cultures in the world but getting down and dirty with the Japanese way was expensive.

The biggest stumbling block to my contribution to a more lucrative income was the need for a proper visa, one which actually allowed me to work, as opposed to the dependent visa, which just allowed me to be here while James worked. And in order to get that coveted passport stamp, I needed a degree. In the late 1980s, the Department of Immigration didn't care what kind of degree you had, as long as you had one. Foreigners with degrees in disciplines as diverse as science, economics, and engineering were happily working their butts off as English conversation teachers in Japan's booming *Eikaiwa*[1] industry.

As part of Mani's homeschooling curriculum, and in an attempt to get him interested in writing, I had suggested that we put together a simple newsletter on topics that interested him about our life in Japan. We planned to send it off to family and friends back home. There were no computers back in the mid 80s that we could use to design and decorate fancy pages with headlines and images. The best we could do in that regard was a gadget called a Print Gokko machine which had just hit the Japanese market. Basically, it was a screen-printing device that worked like a bellows, squeezing an assortment of colored paints through the holes in a postcard-sized screen on which an intense flash of light had burned the design. If it sounds complicated, it was. It took a lot of tweaking, a lot of patience, and a try, try again work ethic, but we managed to produce quite an impressive result. We were both proud of our efforts and the first issue of *The Needle Mouse* (Mani's naming suggestion) went to press in the spring of 1989.

But the Print Gokko machine was destined for far greater, and more dubious, applications. With a little bit of thought and a lot of effort, it became my means to procure a working visa. I'm not going to go into minute detail about how I manipulated the postcard sized device or spent hours in several different 7-Eleven stores wrangling a photocopier to print precise copies of ornate borders onto endless sheets of fancy paper in order to produce an official-looking academic transcript of an undergraduate science degree. To be honest, I was so paranoid about getting caught out doing something dubious, I'm not even sure I remember how I managed it, only that I did.

I was a nervous wreck by the time I visited the immigration office and presented my application for a fully sponsored working visa. I wasn't raised to be dishonest and the subterfuge weighed heavily on my mind. If there had been any other way... but after scarcely a cursory glance at my documentation, the necessary stamp was added to my passport and I became an official Berlitz employee.

But getting the job with Berlitz was only the beginning.

Just as James had done before me, I attended the ten-day training course at head office, and he rearranged his schedule so that he could stay with Mani. On its completion, I was assigned to the Ochanomizu school, which was located in the center of Tokyo. We cleverly arranged our hours to suit ourselves, so that I worked from 8:30 a.m. to 3:10 p.m. on weekdays and all day Saturday, while James worked his regular weekday afternoon shift. It gave me just enough time to catch the train home to Matsudo, meet James at the station, and take over care of Mani. We were like ships in the night, except we passed each afternoon at the same time with the same purpose. By the time he got home after 9 p.m., we were both exhausted, he from his day with Mani and evening with the Berlitz students, and I from my day with different Berlitz students, afternoons with toddlers and their Japanese-speaking mothers, and evenings with Mani.

In hindsight, I wonder how we coped. It should have come as no surprise that our relationship would suffer. Perhaps we didn't have time to notice, but along the way we climbed onto a treadmill, a Möbius strip of English lessons, Japanese lessons, homeschooling lessons, and short breaks out of the country. We simply rinsed and repeated for several years.

JOURNAL

February 20

Today I started work with Berlitz at the Ochanomizu school, slap bang in the middle of Tokyo's student community. I had to do a training course first, as does everyone who works for Berlitz, which meant going into Akasaka every day from 10 a.m. to 4 p.m. James couldn't get any time off while I did the course so he arranged with his head teacher to work from 5:30 p.m. every day I was in training. I got back to Matsudo shortly before that and took over Mani while James went off to work.

I work 8:30 a.m. to 3:10 p.m. every day except Friday and Saturday. Friday is my day off and I use the term loosely because in the morning I have my Japanese lesson and three Friday afternoons a month, I tutor my private group of housewives and their kids. Saturdays I'm open for lessons from 8:30 a.m. to 6:15 p.m. but I don't actually work all that time. So, my schedule is cramped.

Somewhere amongst all this, I have to find time to submit my halfway homeopathy thesis. I needed to read on the train this morning, but it was scarcely possible to stand up let alone read. The pushers were at every door at every station. Unfortunately, until Ochanomizu people only got on not off, so once we reached Ochanomizu it was every man for himself. Whoever said the

Japanese are always polite has never ridden a rush-hour train here. They can be every bit as mean as anyone else.

Our lease is up this month, so we've been busy arranging the renewal. The rent isn't going up, but we have to pay one month's key money, supposedly for renovation, but I'm not sure that they will actually renovate anything but the contract. It's hard to believe we've been here two years already. How time flies.

We had our first big earthquake in ages last night. It was only 5.6 on the Richter scale but loud and thumping, even though it didn't last very long. I often wonder what it would be like to have just arrived at Narita airport and be sitting on the plane waiting to disembark when an earthquake hit. Wouldn't do much for your first impressions of Japan, I imagine.

We're having a mild winter this year. The greenhouse effect is daily news on the BBC now. Already some spring flowers are blossoming, particularly the plum and peach trees. They're beautiful, almost like the cherry blossoms but they're so early. Japan is still ravaging the Southeast Asian rainforests and have just done a back-door deal with Brazil. These are sad and greedy times we live in. Human beings can be so arrogant.

Though I don't particularly agree with it, the Japanese sense of duty is very strong — duty to country, social hierarchy, company, and so on down the chain. It's a big part of their social conditioning, heavily reinforced by the education system. I think it's part of the reason for Japan's postwar success as an industrial power, but it's also responsible for their failure in other domains. It's only now becoming apparent, but crime is on the increase here, though it's still one of the safest countries in the world.

Bullying in schools is a big problem, as is heavy use of corporal punishment for breaking rules that no western school kid would stand for and which, from our point of view, seem unreasonable. In some schools, hairstyles are prohibited, and colors of underwear are inspected. Western media sources often comment on the effectiveness of the Japanese education system but I'm not so sure that's a valid observation. Sure, everyone in this country has a degree, even the fast food shop waitresses and lift attendants; but passing very competitive exams means coughing up cold hard facts that have been obediently swallowed during the last year or so, just like anywhere else. Many students attend a further four hours of cram school every night in order to be *more competitive. It just creates a burden of stress that many kids are not equipped to handle. Hence the high rate of teenage suicide here.*

I'm not saying that the education system I went through was any better, but for different reasons. I was pretty much a vegetable at school as far as creative thinking goes; I was able to come up with reasonable regurgitations of the study cribs at the right time. I failed at university because I didn't see any sense in doing that anymore, I guess. Things you can't learn in schools or universities became more important to me. I have never regretted dropping out of college because my perspectives and values have changed. The education I've had since leaving all those institutions and making alternative choices has been the most valuable. But it can't be measured by grades and certificates.

If I had been able to think, really think intelligently in the true sense of the word, I could have gotten so much more out of an institutional education. That's the kind of advantage we want to give our children. Opportunity comes from strength of mind, the strength of mind it's our responsibility to nurture. It's who you are inside that matters, not where you live or what you do. Security comes from within, not from material wealth. Wisdom comes from experience, not a textbook.

38

SCHOOL DAZE

The Ochanomizu school was fairly large by Berlitz standards and the staff were a mixed bag of nationalities. Apart from two Japanese receptionists and a manager, the rest were foreigners: several Americans and Canadians, a couple of Brits, and a few fellow Aussies. Teachers of languages other than English, like French, German or Spanish, came and went as required, but not often. English was clearly the language in demand, and to teach any language for Berlitz, it had to be your native tongue. Japanese was prohibited in the classroom.

We were all indoctrinated in the Berlitz Method during our induction course. It was based heavily on a question and answer drilling technique using only pictures: no writing, no reading, and no grammar explanations. It was supposed to be conversation only, which worked well with some students. Others, not so much.

We taught most of our lessons one-on-one. Each student had their own pedagogical card on which the teacher recorded the number of the grammar point completed during the last lesson; the next teacher simply picked up from there and carried on. The technique had its strong points, offering absolute beginners the opportunity to start speaking in proper, grammatically correct sentences from the get-go. This gave them confidence and a good sense that they were making progress. Though there wasn't much room for free conversation, as students progressed through each level, it became less like rote learning and more of an inclusive experience.

As with most things though, some people have an aptitude for languages, and some don't. So, some students just couldn't get it, no matter what. Of course, others were just unsuited to the type of learning we were offering, but there was no scope for thinking outside the Berlitz box.

I remember one young woman whose language ability was quite basic. I used to gesture a lot with my hands while I was teaching her, as if that would somehow get the message across more easily. It's the same reason that people speak louder when they feel they aren't being understood. But the only real result of my wild gesticulation was that her head flicked from side to side and up and down as she tried to follow every movement of my hands. It was distracting and unproductive for both of us. In the end, I tried to sit at the table with my hands tucked under my legs for as much of her lesson as possible. It just made me feel like Miss Muffet.

Then there was the student we had nicknamed TS, which stood for The Stutterer. Every teacher had taught the young university student at some point and we all had our opinions about the best way to approach his lesson. He understood our questions completely and was able to answer in perfect, grammatically correct sentences. But getting those sentences out of his mouth took a long, long time. And if you interrupted him or tried to prompt him with the next word, it took even longer because he would start the sentence all over again.

In a 40-minute lesson it was possible to ask about eight questions, or two complete drill sets. His lessons were full of dead air and blank spaces, which we filled by composing shopping lists in our heads or making plans for the weekend. I overheard him speaking to someone on the phone located just outside the office door one day. I was shocked to hear that he was perfectly fluent in Japanese. I wondered if it was his nervousness at speaking English that caused the stutter, but the receptionists confirmed that he was the same with them, even in Japanese. His issue only surfaced in face-to-face situations.

In a lesson themed around careers, I asked him what he would like to do when he graduated from college. It took him around five minutes to tell me, "I would like to be an interpreter with the United Nations!" Then it was my turn to stumble over words.

Individual lessons at Berlitz were expensive, around ¥7,000 ($70) for 40 minutes. Discounts were available for groups of up to six students, but obviously this limited the amount of time that could be spent with each student, who were usually at only roughly the same level of ability. Sometimes the students got lucky and even though they were technically in a group, they were the only ones at that level, so they were able to get individual lessons at group prices.

Each group was allocated a name, usually one of the American states, such as Florida, Texas, or Colorado. The group that struck dread into the hearts of us all was named Washington. Washington consisted of just one student, an elderly lady who had been taking English conversation lessons almost continuously for around ten years. She had been at the school longer than some of the furniture. Her understanding of English was quite good, and her knowledge of grammar put most of us to shame. But her ability to speak in coherent sentences or follow the Berlitz method was seriously flawed.

Not long after I began working at the school, I was scheduled to teach Group Washington for the first of her double lesson time slots. It must have been during the first month of my employment because the head teacher was still periodically monitoring my lessons. A two-way speaker in the ceiling of each room allowed him to listen in and make suggestions if required. He usually only listened. The sudden sound of a random voice coming over the loudspeaker tended to scare the crap out of the students, who knew nothing about the invisible supervision. The head teacher had advised me that this particular lesson was going to be monitored and I was acutely aware that I needed to keep it tight. Washington, on the other hand, wanted to discuss a grammar point.

"Is that a gerund?" she interrupted as I launched into the first question drill of the lesson.

"What? It doesn't matter. Let's just stay with the questions and answers, shall we?" I repeated the question, "Is skiing popular in Japan?" hoping for the full sentence answer, "Yes, skiing is popular in Japan."

"Can you write on the white board, please?" Writing anything, let alone dissecting advanced grammar points with copious written examples was frowned upon.

"Probably best if we just stick to the questions and answers. Do you ski?" I tried a slightly different tactic, still aiming to work back towards the framework of The Method.

"No. Ski? No. I don't like."

"Right. Well, do you think skiing is popular in Japan?"

"This is a gerund. Skiing is a gerund. Why do you call it a gerund?" I'm sure I grimaced. Show me one native English speaker who knows the answer to that question. "Please, write on the board," she reiterated.

"How about you give me a different example? I'm not really supposed to use the white board." I was becoming uncomfortable, and my excuse seemed feeble at best. The sentence I had muttered almost to myself was also probably beyond her level of comprehension. "What about this picture? What are they doing here?" I tapped at the open page of the picture book, trying to redirect her attention and encourage her to think of another word to use instead of skiing. Unfortunately, all the pictures were of people engaged in various high-energy, sporting activities. She wasn't having it. She wanted to show off her grammar skills, and she was right. We were indeed practicing the use of gerunds — verb forms used as nouns. Running, jumping, playing, skiing. I started to wish she would just answer the question. Or that the floor would suddenly open up and swallow me.

Not to be deterred, she rose from her chair, picked up the white board marker herself and wrote the word 'gerund' on the board, and underneath it, 'skiing.' She looked at me expectantly, presumably waiting for some explanation of the term and some further examples. I squirmed in my chair, imagining the head teacher in the roof tearing his hair out and screaming, "No! No! No!" I was sure that any minute now his booming remonstrations would shower both of us. But he remained silent. Minutes stretched out into hours. I had completely lost control of the lesson.

When the end-of-lesson buzzer finally signaled my reprieve, I slunk out the door and down the hallway to the staff room, putting as much distance between me and the head teacher's office as I could. But he came to find me and invited me back to his office for the inevitable debriefing.

"Don't worry. Washington is a difficult customer." He was kind enough to understand. "There wasn't a lot you could have done. She's like that with everyone, even our seasoned experts. Her English level is still quite low even after all the years and buckets of money she's spent on lessons. It's just her way of showing that she does know something. And she's a pleasant woman to teach. Not aggressive like some, at least."

He was right. Some of the businessmen we taught, whose companies were paying for what we called Total Immersion courses, could be downright rude. Usually, they were about to be sent overseas to manage a foreign branch or oversee a new startup, and prior to deployment they would spend a whole week practically tethered to a native speaker. From first lesson in the morning to last lesson at night they were immersed in English, even going to lunch and dinner with a teacher. Their English was often very poor, and they resented what they considered to be a waste of time. And sometimes it was just that. Negative attitudes prevented them from learning anything useful. The teachers didn't enjoy spending time with them either. A 40-minute lesson with them was the equivalent of 80 minutes spent watching paint dry.

There was one other notable category of students. They weren't a large group, but it was pretty obvious they came to English conversation classes purely to increase their chances of landing a foreign husband, or less frequently, a foreign wife. It was easy to tell which ones they were. Though their facial expressions never changed, their shoulders sagged just a little when a teacher of the wrong gender entered their classroom.

From my conversation lessons with the housewives, I had time to observe the life of a Japanese wife. Though there were many positives, some just didn't sit well with my western psyche. I never fully understood why a foreign woman would be interested in marrying a Japanese man. The women may have controlled the purse strings, looked after the home, and raised the kids, but the men still wielded enormous power when they were at home.

A Japanese marriage did not appear to me to be an equal partnership; but looking back now, neither was my own. I was no more in control than they were. The big difference, perhaps, was that they understood their situations, and I was in denial. In my mind, I still believed I was headstrong and independent, even though it was no longer true. My life with James wasn't so different to theirs. I only had a job with Berlitz because he had decided it was his turn to stay home with Mani. He didn't want to work as much, which at the time I accepted as fair. He had worked long hours to support us; it was only right that I should take a turn. But it was his decision that initiated the change.

This inequality in Japanese marriages was brought home to me one afternoon when Mani was invited by *Oni-chan* to visit him at home. We knew that his mother and father were also at home because we could hear them talking to him from our kitchen, which faced onto their garden. As I stood listening with my ear to the back door, I was horrified to hear Mani yell, "Ito-san, you're a snob!" I had no idea what might have prompted him to say such a thing, and I was grateful that they most likely had no idea what he had said. But it spurred me into action, and I went in to rescue them from the antics of a boisterous, foreign toddler.

They were gathered around a *kotatsu* in the front living room when I entered. Although it was a lovely six-mat *tatami* room, glass-fronted cupboards lining the walls limited the available space. The cupboards housed several ornate samurai swords and exquisite figurines in traditional kimono dress. Watching Mani bounce around the room with gay abandon made me extremely nervous.

I was ushered to a cushion at the low table and offered tea. When Ito-san the Mrs. slid open the paper door to the room and prepared to enter, she was kneeling in the hallway. After entering the room, she kneeled again, closed the door behind her and approached the table. She served me first, then her husband, then her son, after which she retreated to the side of the room, knelt again and silently waited. I couldn't believe this was the same woman who graced my *genkan* in street clothes, garden slippers and an apron each month end when our rent was due, and with whom I had engaged in pleasant if basic roadside conversations at their gate whenever we met. No, on this occasion, I was an honored guest and he was the lord of the manor, and there were protocols in place I could scarcely begin to understand. I couldn't imagine myself or any of my freethinking, independent female friends submitting to this level of domestic hierarchy. It was eye-opening.

Interestingly, the Ito's never asked us to become their English teachers, not even for their sons. Given how I had been approached by strangers in public parks and asked to teach, it wouldn't have come as a surprise. Perhaps they were just too polite to intrude on our privacy in our own home. Perhaps that was simply the Japanese way.

I never did work out what had prompted Mani to yell out those four little words that sent me in to their home, and he was too young to remember. It will forever remain a mystery.

39

JOURNAL

March 31

I took an assessment in Japanese at Berlitz today. My private teacher sometimes cancels my lessons and because one of her sons is starting school near Kyoto, she has canceled two weeks in a row. Since Berlitz is cheap for employees, I thought it would be interesting to see what it's like on the other end of the question technique. I now appreciate how important the questions are to the understanding of the material. A few new vocab words for me, drilled correctly, and I picked up the meaning quite quickly. I was pleased that my knowledge of Japanese set me at the beginning of Manual Two, but I hold no illusions as to my conversational ability at this stage. I'm going to try to fit the Berlitz lessons into my schedule because the instant feedback seems to help. But I enjoy Noguchi-san's lessons too, so I'll keep them up as well.

Starting work at Berlitz has brought a big change for me. We've always lived the philosophy that if our child wasn't welcome then neither were we. So, I haven't been separated from Mani for any extended time since his birth. Four and a half years down the track and the transition has been surprisingly smooth. It's been good for both of us. I can't say it's the only way to raise a child, but it has been the best way for us. At the end of the day, everyone has to do what's best for their own family. I've come to see there's no right or wrong way. Parenting is a two-way learning street. Our children teach us just as much as we teach them.

We're in the middle of some strange weather. The cherry blossoms are out about two weeks earlier than usual, and it's raining, tropical style, with intermittent hot and steamy patches. We went to Chidorigafuchi Park after my assessment this morning. It's possibly the most famous Tokyo locale for cherry blossom viewing, and it was certainly beautiful. On the weekends, large groups gather under the trees with ghetto blasters and a microphone to sing karaoke and drink sake.[1] The more sake they drink, the louder they sing, and many of them can't sing a note. They don't seem to notice. Or care. It's hilarious to watch.

But far more impressive, I believe, is Sakura-Dori, a two-mile-long, tree-lined avenue right here in Matsudo. The trees and petals form an archway all along the main street, which leads up to the most amazing temple. We visit this temple often, especially in the fall. The maple leaves transform the grounds into a riot of color almost unbelievable to Australian eyes. We just don't have many deciduous trees back home, so the fourth season is a phantom in most of the country. It's another thing I'll miss when we leave Japan.

40

THE REAL HOUSEWIVES OF MATSUDO AND ICHIKAWA

I've never been one to sit around bone idle or be even just mildly busy. No, there never seems to be enough hours in the day for all I need, and want, to do. Even as a child I burned the candle at both ends, till my parents despaired of their night owl child. Now, with a child of my own, the apple didn't fall far from the tree. He kept me busy till midnight most nights.

So, as well as my full-time job with Berlitz, I continued to teach private lessons outside of school hours. James and I had a highly organized and well-oiled schedule. He stayed with Mani while I worked. Then, on the way home, I met him at the station to collect Mani and he began his afternoon shift. Twice a week, Mani and I went on to private classes with a group of children and their mothers, either in Matsudo or Ichikawa. It was hectic, and though we didn't think much of it at the time, it probably placed undue strain on our relationship. We made it work, but we began to lead separate, though highly integrated lives.

It wasn't hard to pick up work as a private English teacher in Tokyo. Sometimes it involved little more than standing around in the post office or a park with the kids looking like a foreigner, which wasn't difficult. While doing exactly this on a number of occasions, I was approached by women who wanted me to teach either them or their young children, or both. And that's exactly how I became involved with the Real Housewives of Matsudo and Ichikawa.

My mother used to laugh at me for calling them 'The Housewives', but that was how they described themselves. Japanese family life revolved around the husband spending long hours at the office earning the yen, and the wives staying home, cooking, cleaning, raising the children, and spending the yen. The women I taught found this to be quite a congenial arrangement and never questioned it. I think some of them were even grateful for not having to spend too much time with their menfolk.

My Matsudo group laughed together one afternoon while showing me a video of one of the children's birthday parties. Ken-chan's mother had filmed for over 20 minutes, yet in every scene, her husband's head was out of the frame. There wasn't a single image of his face as she panned around the room. One of the women commented, "Takata-san not like husband. Only children." Then they all tittered like birds with their hands over their mouths.

I was quite open to these random job interviews in public places for two very simple reasons. On the one hand, it provided an opportunity for Mani to have contact with children his own age. Having decided not to put him through the agony of the Japanese education system, it was hard to find suitable playmates for him. And on the other hand, it did a similar thing for me — gave me some contact with the world outside our front door, and a wonderful insight into the lives of my adopted countrymen and women.

Though these men and women never became friends of mine in the truest sense of the word, they were as close as I would ever get to having Japanese friends. The lessons I taught were always followed by a couple of hours' conversation around dining tables, half in English and half in Japanese, which was really of more benefit to me than it was to them. I learned more from these unguarded interactions than I did in my weekly coffee shop lesson with my dedicated teacher.

My students and their families were nothing if not generous. They always went above and beyond to help us out. When my parents came over for a visit, they insisted I borrow their car to pick them up at the airport. When I told them of my plans to take my parents on a road trip around Central Japan, they recommended wonderful places to stay, then phoned ahead and made bookings for us at Japanese inns. After my daughter was born, they donated gorgeous, and practically new, baby clothes for her. As a *gaijin*, I must have been exempt from the rule about offering secondhand goods to friends. They invited us for weekend luncheons with their families and treated us like VIPs. But somehow our relationships always remained superficial.

Even as my understanding of Japanese improved in leaps and bounds, they refused to discuss politics, religion, and morality — my three favorite subjects. I discovered that this was directly related to the unwillingness of Japanese people to upset or offend their neighbors in any way. By refraining from voicing an opinion and avoiding the topics that might cause friction or dissent, they managed to keep the peace — and their friends at arm's length. So, our conversations revolved around our children, what we ate, and our travels. It provided me with a window to their Japanese world, and them with a view of the life of a *gaijin*.

I had made it a policy never to set the price of my lessons. I was, of course, bringing a major distraction into the classroom — my son. So, I told my students that my fee was entirely up to them and that whatever they paid me would be gratefully accepted. They never shortchanged me; they were far too honest and generous for that. A couple of times I had to refuse their offers because they were far too high. But generally, it worked out well for both parties. They paid me what they believed the lessons were worth and I was paid more than I would have asked.

I would have taught them for far less than they paid me because it enabled me to spend time on the inside of their society. I got to see how these women lived, how they raised their children, and how they spent their time. They asked lots of questions about my world too, and out of genuine interest. They even came to my home on several occasions and saw how we lived. We shared food and conversation. During our times together, we focused on our similarities, not only our differences. I hope that in some small way I broke down the stereotypical image they had of foreigners, that they came to see, as I did too, that we weren't so different. It was a privilege indeed, and an experience that I was only privy to initially because we had one fundamental thing in common — children.

My interaction with The Housewives lasted until we left Japan. We have since lost contact, but I still remember and think of them with great fondness. They made my life in Japan a joy, probably more than they ever realized. They opened their lives and their homes to me and my children, and I will be forever grateful for their generosity and hospitality.

JOURNAL

May 6

Another day, another page. I'm sitting in a classroom waiting for a student who probably won't turn up since it's already well into his second scheduled lesson. These are called CTLs — cancelled too late. The students have until 3 p.m. the day before their scheduled lesson to cancel and after that they have to pay whether they turn up or not. This week is Golden Week, so-called because of a string of public holidays starting with Emperor Hirohito's birthday on April 29 and ending with Children's Day on May 5. Today is the only working day in the middle of a week of public holidays, so I'm hoping for a few more CTLs.

Last week I was sitting in the post office writing a note to my Japanese teacher when a lady with a young boy approached me and asked me to teach her 'circle'. I decided to accept since she had a couple of kids and didn't mind Mani coming along. I was very glad I did too since she is so lovely, and the kids get on well with Mani. He doesn't have much interface with Japanese kids, so it's good for him. Personally, I'd rather stay home and relax, but he likes to get out and about. Tell me where else you could get paid for taking your son to a friend's house and talking to his mother for a couple of hours. Teaching kids is not easy though, especially ones so young.

Actually, this class was quite a relief. Five non-English speakers can be a real headache. But of this particular five, two are English teachers at cram schools and the others also speak English quite well, so it's possible to have a discussion. I was even surprised to hear Mani speaking Japanese to the kids, the first time this has happened. I commented to my Japanese teacher that he hadn't picked up much of the language, and she said, "Perhaps he's just listening, as babies do, and one day he'll just speak." It's hard to believe he will be five soon. He's been asking about a baby sister or brother lately — he wants two, so he says. Fairies play a big part in his understanding of the world and he wants to know if he asks the fairies to build a baby how long it will take. I would certainly like to have another baby but... there are so many buts.

Mum rang this week with news about Dad and his sudden heart surgery. Unbelievably, she waited a week before calling. He is over the worst now, but I feel torn between wanting to go home and visit with them and waiting till later in the year. I don't have any leave, though this is a valid reason for applying for some. James has suggested that we could arrange it to coincide with our proposed trip to Malaysia and Borneo in August/September. Berlitz has clamped down on extended leave without pay recently but it may make a difference if we say we need extra time due to an illness in the family. It makes sense, but I still feel guilty.

~

42

BEGINNING OF THE END

The year that Dad got sick was probably the beginning of the end of our time in Japan, and it all happened without me knowing anything about it till it was almost over. It started with one of those phone calls. You can tell by the ringtone that something is wrong.

It was early evening in Tokyo when Mum rang from the private hospital in Sydney where Dad had been admitted for coronary bypass surgery. She started the conversation by saying he'd had a funny turn on the golf course. Just like that, with no introduction. In a matter of days, he'd gone from the fourteenth fairway to a theater gurney and come out the other side of a triple bypass operation with a complexion that matched the grey walls of the hospital ward.

"When did this happen?" My voice was just a squeak on the long-distance line.

"About a week ago." Mum apparently didn't think it was worth letting me know sooner. She often delivered verbal blows in a tone that better suited random facts of no real importance.

"Why didn't you call me when it happened?" I couldn't believe I was hearing about this life-threatening event a week after the fact.

"Oh, well, there was nothing you could do from so far away. You probably wouldn't come home even if one of us died anyway." Like so many times before, a flippant comment, delivered so bluntly, shut me down and left me speechless. It wasn't true; it was far from true, and I was stunned that my mother thought it could be true. I told myself that maybe she didn't really think that and was just lashing out because she was scared. I always felt she believed that the choices I had made about where and how I lived my life had all been undertaken with the sole intention of hurting her. But I still couldn't believe she could say something so cruel. My head said fight back, but my heart had already taken a crushing hit. I bit my tongue.

"We don't have any leave right now, but I could probably work something out for later in the year." I heard myself stumble over my reply. As an excuse it sounded pathetic, even to me. Yet again, I felt caught between my husband and my family and found myself making excuses and apologies I neither supported nor believed.

It was true I hadn't been working at Berlitz long enough to have accrued any annual leave, but under the circumstances, I'm sure they would have given me some time off. Australia was a ten-hour flight away and always expensive, even more so at short notice. It didn't seem worthwhile to make the journey for just a few days. I told myself it made more sense to leave it till a later date when we could actually spend more time with our families. But it made no sense not to go at all. This was the story I convinced myself was true.

When James and I discussed our options later that evening we agreed that we could probably include a stopover in Australia when we next left Japan. We had been planning another trip later in the year anyway, to Malaysia and Borneo this time, and visiting the family before or after that would work in quite well. So, James would apply for six weeks' leave so we could fit in the home visit and still have a bit of a vacation.

A stronger person might have not taken that for an answer. A stronger person might have said, "I'd rather go right now." A stronger person might have said, "If you don't want to go, I'll go by myself." And all of those responses might have been quite reasonable in the circumstances. But I wasn't that strong person. Not then. I wanted to see my father, but I didn't have the courage to stand up and say what I really thought. I went along. And I consoled myself with the intention to make things right with everyone when we did visit later in the year. I made excuses and allowances so that, in my mind at least, I began to believe that this was the right decision.

Berlitz granted us a couple of extra weeks because of Dad's illness. But there was another problem, one I hadn't anticipated. The memory of the day James came home with the news that his leave had been approved is still vivid.

"Oh, that's excellent news," I said, relieved that one hurdle was behind us. "Well, I'd better start looking for flight options that include a stopover in Sydney right away. It's hard to get all the connections in place so close to the date we want to fly." Remember, this was before the Internet put travel reservations conveniently in the hands of the masses. In 1989, booking a flight meant shopping around the local travel agencies and making thousands of phone calls to check availability and compare prices. It was a tedious process, and by the time you had enough information to make an informed choice, the situation had often changed. But that wasn't the problem.

"We're not going to Australia." James' tone sounded almost as if he were surprised that I thought so. And he delivered this blow with his back to me. It was a pattern I would come to expect in difficult conversations throughout what was left of our relationship. Maybe he found it easier to break my heart without having to look me in the eye. If I give him the benefit of the doubt, as I often did back in those days, he probably didn't realize how hard those words hit me, or how much they hurt. All the paltry excuses I had forced myself to believe crumbled into pieces. Guilt and resentment replaced them. And anger.

"What? But you got extra leave especially so we could visit Dad." I couldn't believe what I was hearing. I must have gone into shock, the words I should have screamed in response buried in my throat before they were ever uttered. I should have screamed and yelled. I should have fought back. I should have said, "Fuck you!" I should have done a lot of things, not least of which was ignore him and book a flight to Australia for myself and my son.

But hindsight is a wonderful thing. I didn't do any of those things. I was so angry I couldn't bring myself to speak to him for days. But I was angry with myself as much as I was with him. I was the one who wrote all the letters, kept us in contact with friends and family. But I had become his mouthpiece. The words I wrote often bore more resemblance to his opinions than my own. And in the process, his views became mine too. I even believed they were mine. I had let him win a competition that should not have existed. And though it's hard to admit, in doing so I had given up my power, and my voice. Our relationship was no longer a partnership of equals. Somehow, I had reached a point where I didn't feel that I could argue for alternatives. So, this became the status quo.

From where I stand now, it sounds ridiculous. But this is the classic response of a woman locked in a toxic relationship. Abuse doesn't need to be physical to be dangerous. Emotional manipulation is just as powerful and controlling.

Later that year we flew to Malaysia and Borneo as planned. But not Australia. I didn't get to see Dad for another couple of years, when he and Mum finally came over to visit. And worst of all, I never got to explain why to either of them. It probably reinforced their assumption that I didn't care about them. But as was often the case throughout my marriage, I was caught between the proverbial rock and the hard place — defend my husband whom my parents disliked or betray my parents whom my husband disliked.

It came at a price, but I did eventually find the strength to act on my own accord. It took many more years and many more disappointments. But I believe that this denied trip to Australia was the single event that triggered the beginning of the end for our marriage. I wouldn't say it opened my eyes, but it gave me cause to blink.

When we returned from our leave, James insisted I keep the subterfuge alive lest anyone at Berlitz should discover the deception. This meant I had to lie to people, directly and barefaced, something I had been raised to abhor. For some people, lying almost seems to be second nature, and deceit just rolls off their tongues. But for me, not so much. It didn't come easily, and I wasn't very good at it. I felt as if everyone knew I was lying, that my guilt was patently obvious. In my own head, I was humiliated, disappointed in myself for sinking to this level, disappointed that I would abandon my principles so easily and without argument. Again.

∽

43

THE LICENSE TEST AND THE EYE CHART

A pattern developed in our relationship that when difficult issues arose, we focused on something else. So, the subject of the missed trip to Australia wasn't mentioned again. Even I acted as if nothing had happened, as if nothing had been lost. But in my heart, I resigned myself to a defeat I couldn't properly articulate or understand. The seeds of resentment took hold.

I buried my disappointment by working endless hours and raising my son. I should have brought it up. I should have made it matter more. But *should have* has no value in the present. Nothing can be changed by realizing what *should have* been said or done. Still, something was gone, something important.

Because we usually left Japan for our vacations, we hadn't actually seen much of our adopted home in the time we had been here. So, it became obvious that if we hoped to see any more of the country than the area serviced by the subway system, we were going to either have to hire a car or buy one; and that was going to require a license. Our international driving permits would soon expire, so the only avenue left was to swap them for official Japanese ones, known as *unten menkyo*. Even the words sounded like a rare, exotic disease. But the

The License Test and the Eye Chart 185

Unten Menkyo Center in Chiba Prefecture, where we lived, was a law unto itself.

We managed to fill out the necessary forms, in triplicate, after learning to recognize the *kanji* characters for name, address, date of birth, etc. But the real fun began with the eye test. I was ushered into a small room where I found myself alone with a large, metal, electronic box fitted with a pair of binoculars similar to those you might find at a scenic lookout.

Two female staff soon joined me and went to great pains to carefully explain the instructions while I nodded and said, *"Hai,"* at frequent and appropriate intervals. Actually, I understood only a few scant details, but it seemed rude to say so, not to mention inconvenient. The first rule of living in Japan was to avoid saying no at any cost. It was right up there with bowing.

I put my face up to the little binoculars at the top of the box, and peered in. I was confronted with a backlit chart of circles about six columns wide and twenty rows long. Each little circle had a gap on one side, like the letter c, but facing all different directions. From the instructions, I guessed that I had to say where on the chart the lit-up circle appeared, so I blithely rattled off the words for top, bottom, left, and right depending on where on the chart it occurred. I didn't have time to wonder at the lack of demarcation between the various columns when answering. After several attempts, I could tell from the looks on the faces of my testers that I was getting every one of them wrong. They looked at me sympathetically, as if I must have been either completely blind or completely stupid.

Then the penny dropped. I was not supposed to say where on the chart the circle was located, but rather the direction the gap was facing. The same answers still applied — top, bottom, left, right — but the reasoning behind them was completely different to the logic I had been using. I begged, in my best Japanese, to be permitted to start over, and while they looked as if they thought that was going to be a pointless exercise, they agreed.

This time I got them all right and my examiners breathed an audible sigh of relief. They even commended me on my visual acuity. We all bowed deeply, relieved the ordeal was over.

Before James went in for his test, I had about ten seconds to brief him so he could avoid making the same mistake I had. We finally left the office several hours later, proud holders of official *unten menkyo*. As it turned out, those tiny squares of laminated officialdom opened more doors for us than just the driver's side of the car. We had finally arrived in Japan, just seven years after landing at Narita International Airport one soggy, April afternoon.

∽

1990

44

ROBBED

One of the more unsettling things that happened to us during our time in Nakayagiri was a break-in. I could hardly say we were robbed since nothing was actually taken. We came home mid-afternoon to find the place a mess. Nothing unusual there, but then I noticed that all our drawers had been emptied out and their contents were strewn across the floor. You become accustomed to chaos when one of the occupants of the house is a 5-year-old, but this was clearly more than that. It was the work of a burglar.

It was a bit of a shock. You never think it will happen to you. The intruder had smashed one of the windowpanes in the spare room and come in across the *tatami* with his shoes on, leaving a couple of muddy prints and a few broken reeds. Our passports had been removed from the money belt, but thankfully abandoned.

Since my Japanese had improved to the point where I could now hold more than a polite conversation about the weather or pay for my groceries, I decided to inform the police. So, I phoned the local police box, which was located underneath the platforms at Matsudo station. Three policemen in immaculate navy uniforms arrived within the hour. On bicycles. Yes, even the constabulary use bikes to get around.

They brought a fingerprint guy with them and he set about dusting all the flat surfaces, finding mostly grubby hieroglyphics painted by Mani. They probably thought the intruder had messed the place up pretty badly, but in truth, most of the mess was of our making. The thing that struck me as strange was that they didn't have a camera. One of the policemen sat down at our dining table and proceeded to draw diagrams of everything that had been touched, complete with indicators as to where the fingerprints were located. They stayed for a couple of hours, interviewing us, drawing pictures, and leaving no stone unturned in their investigation of the facts.

A couple of days later, I received a phone call from one of the attending officers. He wanted to go over my statement one more time. He said I had reported the time at which we arrived home as approximately 3:30 p.m. but they had arrived at the scene of the crime at 4:00 p.m. He explained to me that this time frame didn't add up, since I had also said that I phoned in about an hour after we arrived home. For want of another option, I suggested that I must have got it wrong and that we had actually arrived home at 3:00 p.m. It wasn't exactly true, but this minor adjustment to my story made him extremely happy, and he hung up.

It was probably about six months later that a car pulled up out the front of our house and two plain clothes detectives knocked at the door. They explained that they had arrested the gentleman waiting in the car on several counts of robbery and following his confession, he was now taking them on a tour of all the places he had robbed over the last few months. They just wanted to confirm that we had indeed been robbed. Evidently, this is the Japanese way — confession followed by a guided tour of the crime scenes.

We never found out what his punishment was, but they did inform us that he was probably after drivers' licenses or insurance documents, neither of which he had found. He must have been the only person in Matsudo who did not know that this was the house where the *gaijin* lived.

45

PARENTAL VISIT

Mum and Dad finally came over to visit in April 1990. We were more or less successful in timing their visit to coincide with the cherry blossoms, although it was cut short that year by unseasonal rain. The astonishing beauty of the Japanese seasons never ceased to amaze and delight us, coming, as we do, from a land where the seasonal demarcations are defined more by temperature than anything else.

The Ichikawa Housewives had very graciously loaned us a car to drive out to the airport to collect Mum and Dad. Narita is a good 40 miles from Tokyo and it's difficult to navigate the rail system with luggage. Heck, it's even difficult to navigate the spaghetti soup that is the Japan Rail system without luggage. But this was the first time I'd ever driven in Japan. I was driving someone else's car, unused to the narrow roads, and not at all fluent in the *kanji* required to read road signs. Thank God they drive on the same side of the road as we do in Australia.

Riding around the streets and back alleys of the suburbs on two wheels, I'd had little reason to take notice of which of them were big enough for vehicular traffic, or even which were one-way. It was a baptism of fire for me, but it spared Mum and Dad from having to ride a jam-packed train immediately after their long flight.

Our little house seemed so much smaller and crowded with two extra people inside. Each time we returned from vacation, I realized how low the ceilings actually were, how small and box-like the rooms. They were built for people shorter in stature than either of us. Seeing my tallish father standing in the living room made it that much more obvious. Coupled with this, Mum and Dad had to deal with taking off their shoes, putting on the toilet shoes in the bathroom, sleeping on *futon* on the floor, and coping with the frenzied antics of a demanding five-year-old grandson whom they hardly knew.

It wasn't long before Mum tired of Mani's behavior, or misbehavior as she saw it, and decided to share her thoughts on how it should be dealt with. We had always been judged negatively for our apparent lackadaisical attitude to childrearing and discipline, but now we were on home ground and I felt emboldened by that fact.

"Do you want me to tell you what I think you should do?" Mum had been silently watching Mani bounce around the lounge room full of beans for some time. I could sense her growing disgruntlement and indignation.

"Actually, no," I responded. "This is a very small space and we all have to live together and get along for the next month, so I think it's probably best if you keep your opinions to yourself."

Dad smiled to himself and hid his face in his cup of tea. In hindsight, I was amazed at the directness of my quick retort. The me my mum knew had always been a peacekeeper, the one who listened, tightlipped, while someone told me what they thought. I didn't necessarily agree with what they said, but I didn't have the will to argue. Perhaps motherhood had changed me more than I thought, but when my parenting skills were called to account, I had plenty of defense in the tank and plenty, it seemed, to defend. But this time, it had the desired effect. She never broached the subject again.

Meals were another source of discomfort for Mum and Dad. They'd always been meat and two veg people, which didn't fit well with either a Japanese menu or our vegan lifestyle. James and I had made the switch to a plant-based diet early in our stay in Japan. It was just so easy here. I took on the Japanese housewife's habit of shopping each day for fresh ingredients, and with tofu and soy products so readily available and so tasty, we didn't want for choice. While I was a stay-at-home mum, I had had all the time in the world to prepare meals, necessary if one intends to remain fit and healthy on a vegan diet. Things had changed a lot since I started teaching at Berlitz, but we still ate well. It didn't help that I took the hard line of refusing to have meat in the house with Mum and Dad.

We couldn't even solve this problem by going out for dinner. The restaurants that catered for meat-eaters had little to offer James and me. And the restaurants that could accommodate us specialized in traditional Japanese fare. Meals together became a nightmare. One time, I actually resorted to helping Mum and Dad choose one of the plastic model meals in the window of one restaurant and then going to the one next door to order for us.

My housewife students came to the rescue when I was planning things we could do with Mum and Dad to show them a good variety of experiences in our adopted home country. They not only recommended places for us to go, they also rang up and booked accommodation for us around our planned itinerary. And they turned out to be excellent choices.

We hired a car for the trip and wound our way down the extensive, and expensive, freeway network in the direction of Kyoto, stopping on the way at Kanazawa and Takayama. The housewives had booked us a lovely *onsen* experience in Kanazawa. We had a huge, traditional *tatami* mat room with an amazing view across the mountains, access to the hot baths, and dinner and breakfast for all of us.

Dinner was served directly to our room. Two kimono-clad waiters knocked and entered the room with a flourish of crockery, cutlery, and steaming dishes. We took our seats on cushions around the low table and they set places before each of us, explaining the contents of each dish as they did so. I did my best to translate what was being served. When they had covered the table with exquisite Japanese crockery and dishware, they removed the lids to reveal their steaming contents.

As each dish was unveiled, the look on Mum's face changed from intrigue to horror. Snuggled in the bottom of the last beautiful blue bowl was a tiny *tako*.[1] She looked at me aghast.

"What is it?" she asked.

"I believe it's octopus." I knew exactly what it was. There was no point trying to sugar coat it.

"Well, I guess I'll have to wait till breakfast for something to eat." She'd already made up her mind that there was nothing here for her. Dad didn't appear to be much more impressed with some of the dinner offerings than Mum, but he had always been more open to trying different things. He made a good show of tasting all the dishes, with the notable exception of the octopus delicacy. He even had a go at using the *hashi*.[2] He may not have been blown away by the banquet, but at least he didn't go hungry.

Mum didn't fare any better at breakfast time. Served in the hotel restaurant this time, we sat down to a traditional Japanese breakfast of miso soup, pickles, fried fish, rice, and an egg. Mum's eyes lit up at the sight of the familiar item that at last meant she could eat. Eagerly, she picked it up to begin shelling it just as I remembered an important fun fact. The egg served with a Japanese breakfast is eaten with the rice — raw! But I was too late. The shell shattered on the edge of the bowl, spilling its gooey contents all over the table and placemat.

Very soon after that, we paid our bill and left for Kyoto, via the nearest coffee shop serving recognizable food.

The stunning temples and gardens of Kyoto never fail to impress, and they did seem to make up in some small part for Mum's culinary disappointment. Kinkakuji and Ginkakuji, the famous gold and silver pagodas, the Philosopher's Walk, and the remarkable manicured gardens did the job. It was a visual feast if not a gastronomic one. And the cherry blossoms were now in full flower, adding their delicate pink mist to the landscape.

As we drove out of town towards Arashiyama, an outlying suburb that boasted a mountain lookout frequented by macaque monkeys, we passed a particularly impressive grove of hanging cherry blossoms. Huge branches hung like willows over pebbled pathways, showering visitors with pale pink splendor. I caught Mum resting her legs on a large marble seat, one of many of various sizes dotted throughout the garden. Then I noticed Dad, off to the side, trying to conceal his obvious glee as he shot image after image on his camera.

"How cute!" I said as I came up behind him.

"Do you see what she's sitting on?" He motioned in Mum's direction, a huge smile on his face.

From the short distance away, I suddenly realized what we were looking at. The black marble statue fashioned into a seat was actually a giant penis, the shaft forming the backrest and two testicles in front acting as the seat. Oh, the horror! Mum was the ultimate prude, and if she only knew where she had chosen to sit, the earth would no doubt have opened up and swallowed her. Dad and I looked at each other and doubled over in stitches.

"Let's not tell her!" We agreed it was probably for the best.

A few days later, armed with only a few phrases that I thought might come in handy, plus a few more Dad thought to ask about at the last minute, we saw them off on the *Shinkansen* for Nagasaki in the far south of Japan. They would be on their own for a week. And so would we.

∽

46

ZEN AND THE ART OF TRAIN TRAVEL

*R*iding the Japanese train system, both the subway and the above ground, is an art, especially if one wishes to survive without being crushed. And deciphering the strings of colored spaghetti and hieroglyphics that represent the 13 different Tokyo subway lines and stations almost requires a master's degree in engineering. During peak hours, men with dark blue uniforms and white gloves have the odious task of pushing everyone into the carriages so that the doors can fully close or pulling people off the train to enable them to disembark. It's not easy, and even worse on rainy days when most commuters are carrying umbrellas. Sometimes it takes more than one of them to complete the task.

As you might expect, Japanese train stations are highly organized. Loudspeakers constantly remind passengers, "Because it's dangerous, please stand behind the yellow line." Other markers on the platform indicate precisely where the carriage doors will be when the train stops. And they always are. So, waiting passengers queue in two orderly lines at each of the markers. All is calm, until the train arrives. Then it becomes tricky. Passengers standing in the train doorway when the doors open are forced to alight from the carriage to allow those who actually want to get off at this stop to do so. But, immediately after the disembarking passengers are out, the people at the back of the waiting line begin to run towards the doors, pushing those in front of them either into the carriage or sideways along the edge of the carriage, away from the doors. So, it can happen that the people who were at the front of the queue end up not being able to get on the train.

The day Mum and Dad rode their first train, early in their stay, they were convinced that the whole population of their small hometown were in the carriage with them. We had no choice but to stand in the door area because there were no seats anywhere and the aisles were already full. This meant that when the train stopped, Mum, who was pole hanging near the door, needed to get off and back on again as described above. The only problem was, she didn't know that, so she clung to the pole as the rest of the town tried to get off the train around her.

"Mum! Let go! Get off the train!" I tried calling to her but to no avail. She was terrified, and she couldn't understand why on earth she should get off the train. Eventually, those who needed to got off, and those waiting outside got on, and the whole process repeated itself at every station along the way with Mum still clinging to the central pole for dear life. She was lucky she had the pole for security, because the rest of us, with nothing to hang onto, all obeyed Newton's first law of motion and continued forward as the train decelerated, until we leaned on top of each other at a precarious 45-degree angle.

With trains this crowded, groping by strangers was a real issue. Several of my colleagues at Berlitz reported being felt up on the way to work by hands that couldn't be identified. Coupled with the up close and personal study of the blemishes and skin texture on the neck of the man or woman standing beside you, commuting was not much fun. For all these reasons, I quit working in the city on weekdays when I was about six months pregnant and worked only on Saturdays, when the commute was more bearable. Otherwise, it was just too dangerous. Even being heavily pregnant did not entitle one to a seat.

∼

47

PREGNANT AGAIN

The night that Mum and Dad left to return home was a bit of a relief. Not because we didn't enjoy having them visit and showing them around our adopted homeland. Mostly it was because we lived in such a small space, and sharing it, even with members of our own family, placed a strain on all of us. Perhaps more so for them. In the West, we take our personal space for granted in lots of ways, and in Asia it's a luxury that just doesn't exist. I found myself constantly reminding Mum and Dad that there was someone behind them, or trying to pass, and their lack of awareness of reduced physical space made things awkward.

They had survived a lot: sleeping on futons on the floor, constantly putting on and taking off shoes, trains so crowded you couldn't get on or off, strange inedible offerings at restaurants, a visit to Disneyland with a five-year-old (eek!), and sharing a small space with the same demanding five-year-old. Their departure allowed us to relax a little again and spend some quiet time together. We relaxed so much, in fact, that I fell pregnant with our second child that very night.

I knew I was pregnant right away. Don't ask me how. I just did. I wasn't ready to give up working at Berlitz immediately. Besides, I was taking cheap Japanese language lessons at the school in my spare time and loving it. We had to consider our options for the birth, too. After my experience with the fate of my last pregnancy and the Japanese medical system, there was no way I was going to give birth in a local hospital.

I kept working at Berlitz until I was around six months along. It gave me plenty of time to plan for the birth. It became obvious that a home birth wasn't going to happen in Japan, not without taking a huge risk. I wasn't even game to mention it to my Japanese doctor, and when he began discussing the delivery schedule and possible outcomes, I knew it was going to mean a trip back home to Australia. The Japanese medical system was neither supportive of nor geared up for homebirth, and having successfully birthed my son at home in Taree with only a midwife present, I was not prepared to compromise. The importance of the birth process was central to my philosophy on childrearing, and I could only foresee disaster by staying in Japan.

Along with the usual concerns about how long I could leave it before I was no longer allowed to fly, there was the issue of where to go, where to stay, and which midwife to engage. The beautiful lady who had delivered Mani was now living in an alternative community in Byron Bay, an area of the northern New South Wales coast fast becoming known for its burgeoning hippie population and expensive summertime accommodation. With the help of a local real estate agent, we managed to find a reasonably-priced apartment in town, but three weeks before our departure, it fell through. The alternative we were offered didn't sound great, but at that point we had little choice. And the price was right.

At the last minute, we secured a ground floor two-bedroom apartment in the village of Suffolk Park for around $200 a week. It was the first floor of a two-story beach house, but the owner who lived upstairs was planning a trip to Melbourne for most of the time we would be there. That part was perfect. As it turned out, so was the location.

∽

48
JOURNAL

September 3

Breaking news. We are having another baby. I've been seeing a crazy Russian doctor at the international clinic in the city and everything seems to be fine this time. I've been getting a lot of kicks, earlier than I remember with Mani. The baby is due on January 6. I'm only working Saturdays at Berlitz from now on. It's difficult to take rush-hour trains, but Saturday is not so crowded. I still have my kids' class in Ichikawa, which I'm thinking of cutting back to once a week, and the dentist in town has changed his schedule so that he can continue to take his lessons. He really enjoys them. Last lesson he told me he'd closed the practice the day before in order to go to a bargain shoe sale. He likes to take things easy.

Rosie, the midwife I had for Mani's birth, is going to attend again, so we are definitely going to Australia. I'm planning to do another meditation course at the Blackheath Vipassana center as soon as we arrive in late November. James has about two-and-a-half months' leave from Berlitz. He's been working longer hours since I quit weekdays to make up some of the difference. It's going to be an expensive trip, but infinitely preferable to having a baby in Japan. There are midwife centers here but most of the midwives running them are elderly and very conservative. Communicating our wishes to them would be difficult to say the least. New Year births are rumored to cost around ¥1 million (very inconvenient time as everyone is on vacation). It will be very strange to be home again after four years. I guess a lot of things will have changed.

It's starting to get cold here now. Tokyo is wet and rainy, and we have the heater on. Mani is off playing somewhere but he's been awfully quiet for too long, which usually means he's up to no good.

I changed doctors a couple of weeks ago. I found out that the crazy Russian I was seeing was up to his neck in malpractice suits spanning ten or fifteen years, filed by the American gynecologist I saw at the same clinic some time ago. My new guy is British and very, very nice. He insisted on doing every single test all over again and decided that I only need a B12 injection, as my B12 is on the low side of the normal range. When I told him I was a vegan he was very interested and asked me why, rather than the usual question I get, which is, "What on earth is that?" He almost convinced me to stay in Japan for the birth, but I couldn't find any friendly midwives in this area.

We will be arriving in Sydney on November 19. We'll spend a day in Sydney before heading up to Blackheath so I can do the meditation course. James and Mani will stay somewhere in Katoomba till the course finishes, then we'll head up north together, hopefully by train, since the buses scare the hell out of me after those recent horror smashes on the Pacific Highway.

The plans after that are a little sketchy. The house Rosie found for us has fallen through because the owners are looking for long-term tenants, but we have found another place from December 6 to around January 20. Once the baby is born, we will have to move fast to get all the paperwork done in time to get back to Japan before our 90-day tickets expire. No one sells discount flights for any longer than that. There are so many complications and considerations that I really wish there were a way to stay here for the birth. I went to a childbirth exercise class in Tokyo last week hoping they might be able to help me with some fresh ideas, but we live in an awkward part of town — remote, they call it.

Still quiet on the Mani front. Better stop writing this and go check.

∽

49

ALMOST HOME

Not content with making a meal out of the arrangements for the birth and the flights back home, I also decided that I wanted to do another Vipassana course before my baby arrived, just as I had done when I was pregnant with Mani. The center I had attended in the Blue Mountains when pregnant with Mani was holding a course that coincided exactly with the date of our arrival in Sydney. So, I applied and was accepted into the ten-day course. For a mum about to give birth, it's a special opportunity to spend a lot of time with her unborn child. I highly recommend it. At least one Vipassana course should be mandatory for all expectant mothers, in my humble opinion.

The next ten days were spent in silent introspection, sitting cross-legged in a dimly lit hall. We sat like this for ten to twelve hours a day but every so often, as an old student (anyone who has previously completed a ten-day course), I was allowed to meditate in the newly completed pagoda. It was much cooler, and I had a small 'cell' all to myself, which made the meditation so much more focused. It was a powerful experience and one I remember fondly to this day.

After the completion of the meditation course, I was reunited with James and Mani and we caught the train to Byron Bay via a short stop in Taree to catch up with family. I remember the rail journey as a day of very high temperatures, so high that the railway tracks had expanded and buckled in places, making it necessary for the train to crawl along at a snail's pace. We were all fed up with trains by the time we arrived in the beachside town, the end of the line at the time.

I had long lost relatives living in Byron, an aunt and cousins I hadn't seen in years. Even though the train arrived several hours late, they very kindly met us at the station and transported us to our rented accommodation in Suffolk Park, a few miles to the south of the famous lighthouse on the Cape. The landlord greeted us, then left us alone to get settled in. It had been a long, tiring day and we were very grateful.

The next morning, we discovered how perfect our new home really was. At the bottom of the back yard, a narrow path led straight to the beach. It couldn't have been more than 30 steps. Mani was in his element, co-opting the backyard washing trolley into a torturous game of push-me-pull-you up and down the wet sand. The beach was clean and golden, and the waves shone with the excitement of the Australian summer sun. Dad always used to say you could tell a good beach by the way it squeaked as you plunged one foot after another into it as you trekked across the warm sand. This one was certainly a candidate for that category. Standing ankle-deep in the shallows looking all the way up the coastline to the Cape Byron lighthouse, it was a sight to behold in the early morning mist. We were all in love.

On our way through Taree, we had collected a host of items that had been stored at Mum and Dad's place since we moved to Japan. Most of them were electrical appliances and soft furnishings that we could not take with us. We planned to sell them off at the local markets in Byron. The pre-Christmas timing would hopefully make it an ideal venue.

The day of the markets demanded an early start for the three of us. We caught a taxi to the showground at around 6 a.m., only to find a long line of cars already waiting to get through the gates. Some early birds had made it through and were busily setting up their stalls in highly controlled, designated spots. We had no alternative but to join the end of the line and wait — two adults, one of them heavily pregnant, one child, two large suitcases, and no car. Just us and the bags standing in a line of cars. Each time the queue progressed, we each grabbed a suitcase and moved forward with the rest. If it looked ridiculous, it was nothing compared to how I felt. At one point, James rushed off to check on the protocol for the day with the people in charge at the head of the line, leaving me and Mani to cope with the overladen bags. I tried not to make eye contact with anyone sitting in the cars ahead of or behind us. It was just too humiliating.

It was a rocky start to the day, and by the time we were directed to our allocated spot on the field and spread out our assorted wares, I was ready to just give everything away to anyone who offered a cursory glance as they passed. It was hot by 9 a.m., there was no shade, and we were spending our takings on drinks and popsicles faster than we could collect it. But the people came, saw, and purchased with relative frequency so that by lunch time almost everything was sold. We gave the few remaining items to friends who happened to visit at the right time, and left with about $100 more than when we arrived. We ditched the empty bags in the nearest dumpster and walked back into town to get some well-earned refreshments. When I look back on that day, I still can't believe that I survived it.

Despite the hardships that were part of the journey, I grew to love Byron more over the next few weeks. I found a renewed love for the country I used to call home and began to dream of moving back in the not too distant future. We had plenty of money in the bank that could serve as a deposit on a home, and prices were still at pre-boom levels. It was a fantasy I had a hard time constraining. I had seen the world, not all of it, but enough to know that I was ready to come home, and Byron looked like a great place to call home.

We truly do come from a lucky country and my travels in other parts of the world had made me realize that and appreciate it. But James didn't feel the same way. He still nursed a longing to be somewhere else, anywhere other than Australia, and he resisted my suggestions by simply failing to discuss them in any real depth.

In hindsight, and for me the real estate market is only ever understandable that way, buying property would have been the best thing we could have done. We were still too young and naive to understand that buying property is probably the best thing you can do, ever. We would have made a fortune out of even a small investment in the far north coast of New South Wales. But we didn't. And sometimes, in the dark of night, when I lie awake chasing sleep around an endless loop, that failure to act with the future in mind still niggles at me, even thirty years down the track.

50

BIRTHING POOL

Without our own means of transportation, we were at the mercy of a regional and very sketchy bus service from the village of Suffolk Park into town, a trip of about seven kilometers. There was only so far we could go without wheels and clearly it was too far for me to walk, though in non-pregnant days I wouldn't have thought twice about the inconvenience.

My relatives once again came to the rescue. My aunt very kindly let us borrow her little red car so that we could get out and explore the area for a day. And there was lots to see.

After dropping her back at her apartment in town, James drove us out towards Mullumbimby, one of Byron's smaller hinterland towns. From there, we were spoilt for directions. Every road seemed to lead to sparkling waterfalls and natural deep water swimming holes. One of the roads we chose wound its way up into the hills, past homes straight out of my dreams, properties that seemed to hang from the trees in midair, lovingly crafted by people with only themselves in mind. Handmade homes that suited the environment and their owners.

The deeper into the forest we went, the more the road deteriorated, until it was just a rutted track barely wide enough for two vehicles to pass. Driving too fast over a particularly bumpy section, we hit a large rock that appeared and disappeared almost before we had time to see it, let alone avoid it. There was a loud thump.

"What was that?" I clutched the door handle in anticipation of suddenly being launched through the windscreen. It didn't happen.

"I have no idea." James laughed almost hysterically, gripping the steering wheel as if his life might soon depend on it. In the rear seat, Mani whooped and shrieked with delight at the sudden upturn the adventure had taken, oblivious to the danger.

"There's a light. What's that? Should I stop?" I looked over at James. He was staring wild-eyed at the dashboard where a single red light stared back, unblinking, like a silent accusation.

"Stop?" I exclaimed with great alarm. "Are you mad? We're in the middle of nowhere and I'm about to have a baby any minute. Do you really think that's a good idea?" I patted my swollen belly to make sure it was still there.

James looked at me aghast. "No, you're right. Guess not."

He kept driving, and after several minutes that felt more like days, we came upon the outskirts of Uki and the start of the sealed road. Just as the front wheels hit the tarmac the engine died, and we coasted toward the intersection with the main road to Casino and Murwillumbah. That was it. The engine was cooked. Not even a click when the key was turned. It had pretty much welded itself together.

"Now what?" We sat in silence for a little while, pondering the consequences of what we had done.

"I guess we better call someone," I said. "Do you see a phone box anywhere round here?"

James pointed in the direction of the pub about 50 yards down on the opposite side of the road. "Look! There's one just over there," he said, and headed off while I waited on the corner with Mani.

The NRMA mobile assistance van driver who arrived a couple of hours later couldn't believe it. "How far did you drive with the oil light on?" he asked, shaking his head before he even heard the answer.

"Oil light? A few kilometers, I guess," James replied.

"That was kind of my fault," I offered, pointing at my belly. Neither of us had any real knowledge of car engines, and even less experience with things that could go wrong. And to be fair, we *were* in the middle of the forest, and I *was* about to give birth. It was a risky journey to have made, given the circumstances. But none of those excuses were of any use when I had to break the news to my aunt. She was understandably devastated.

We organized for the car to be towed back to Byron and waited another hour or so for a tow truck to arrive. The driver who turned up was a surly man, not happy to be called out so late on a Sunday afternoon. He only had room in the cab for one of us and wasn't well-disposed towards taking James back to the garage in Murwillumbah with him. He seemed to resent the fact that we had called him at all and decided to be difficult.

We thought it best to stick together, and the three of us followed him back in a taxi. It was an expensive ride into town, for us and the little red car, but one that couldn't be avoided. It was well after dark when we got home. And it was our last trip out of Suffolk Park for quite some time.

We paid for a new engine to be fitted, but the car was never the same according to my aunt. I felt worse than ashamed, but the damage was most definitely done. Nothing else we could do now would improve the dreadful outcome. We had been irresponsible, and someone else had paid the price. It was awful.

After the accident, our days were divided between shopping for groceries in the local IGA supermarket and lazing around on the beach. The midwives came and went periodically just to check how things were going. But the due date came and went with no sign of the baby.

One morning when Rosie called in, she brought the local home birth book. It was a hardcover foolscap notebook in which all the local home birth mums had written their birth stories, along with sketches, doodles, and photographs. Reading them was inspiring and Rosie encouraged me to keep it until after the birth and write up our own story.

Around this time, the possibility of a lotus birth[1] was raised. I have to confess that when it was first described to me, I was repulsed. But once it was properly explained and my many questions answered, I started to warm to the idea. We had already gone out on a limb by deciding to have a water birth at home. Why not go for the full hippie experience? When in Rome, as they say.

There were still lots of arrangements to be made. I can't remember who loaned us the birthing pool, but from the day it arrived until the day my parents came for a visit, it sat in the middle of the spare bedroom in a deflated heap. For the life of me I couldn't work out how to attach the vacuum cleaner so that it blew air in rather than sucking it out. So, I turned to the person who always knew what to do — Dad.

It was a standing joke in our family that Dad's real name was Mr. Right and his middle name was Always. He liked to be right, and he liked to win. Reluctantly, he sorted out the birth pool. He didn't like the idea of a water birth one little bit and felt that by helping me inflate the pool he was giving his tacit approval. Aiding and abetting were the actual words he used. But he still did it, God love him.

Once it was blown up it took up a lot of space. And it also took a lot of water to even half fill it. We dragged in a garden hose to get the level up to halfway and the midwives conditioned the water with special, body-friendly products. The plan was to leave it that way until the birth was imminent, then complete the fill with hot water in order to bring it up to body temperature. It turned out to be another of our flawed plans.

The morning before our baby arrived, I swam with dolphins. It wasn't planned that way but in Byron Bay even the dolphins are hip. Three of them just happened to be surfing the waves right out the back of our beach house. They swam close to me as I wallowed in the waves, not quite close enough to reach out and touch, but I felt an amazing sense of peace and calm as they circled. Though I didn't know it at the time, this very special event heralded my daughter's birthday.

Everyone went to bed early that night. Even me. But by 1 a.m., I was swinging from the bathroom architrave trying to relieve the pressure and pain in my lower back. My antics woke my sister-in-law who was sleeping in the spare room, the one where the birthing pool stood idle, still only half-filled with cold water. Emerging in a sleep haze, she enquired whether she should start filling it. Abruptly, and in a tone that only a woman about to give birth can muster, I ordered her to wake James, tell him to phone the midwives, and then fill the bath — the one in the bathroom.

We didn't have a phone in the beachside apartment. In the early 90s, mobile phones were still the size of house bricks and weighed about the same. They were far from truly mobile and horrendously expensive. Phoning the midwives meant that James had to get on a bicycle and ride down the road in the dark to the nearest public phone, about 500 yards away. One of the midwives lived nearby, but the other was about half an hour's drive away, on the other side of Byron. By the time she arrived, she was almost too late.

I chose to lie face down in the bath because it allowed the water to support me and reduce the pain of the contractions. I was almost able to float, but not quite. I couldn't completely stretch out either, but it was so comfortable that I absolutely refused to turn over, making it extremely difficult for Rosie to monitor progress. Consequently, Noa was born face up in the fairly shallow water. We had hoped she would remain underwater immediately after her birth, but her nose broke the surface and she drew her first breath sooner than expected.

The lotus birth we had decided on meant that we didn't cut the cord that attached baby to placenta. The midwives dried it then treated it with salt and wrapped it securely in towels. It became 'the package' that stayed with Noa until it simply dried, shriveled, and fell away. But that didn't happen for three days, and when it did, it brought with it a most amazing experience for me and my baby daughter.

I was used to being the main caregiver for my family, so when the super high energy level that follows a birth kicked in, I became a human dynamo, cooking, cleaning, breastfeeding, bathing, baby massaging, staring into my newborn's eyes, and occasionally sleeping. Eventually, it took its toll and on the third day after the birth I fell victim to milk fever. It struck in the early evening as I was washing the dinner dishes. Rosie had just arrived and, seeing me working away at the sink, demanded to know why I wasn't resting.

"Well, I have all this energy, but I do suddenly feel a bit tired, and a little squeamish if I'm honest," I admitted. "Things still need to get done, though."

"Yes, you have a lot of extra energy, but it's meant for the baby, not for housework." She insisted that I go and lie down with the baby immediately. Obediently, and glad to get away from the kitchen sink, I did as I was told. As I lay down on the bed where Noa lay sleeping, she opened her eyes and looked deeply into mine. Waves of love poured over me.

Still looking at me and ever so purposefully, she reached up with her left foot, grabbed the dried-up cord between her tiny toes and pulled it free from her. Instantly, my nausea and fever disappeared. The process was complete. She was really here.

We placed the placenta package into the freezer until we could decide what to do with it. It would have been nice to plant it together with a small tree sapling as we'd done with Mani's six years earlier. But this was just rented accommodation that we would likely never visit again. Noa had been born in the sign of Aquarius, so it seemed only fitting to return it to the sea. We had a small ceremony on the beach the night before we left the house, thanking Mother Nature for the wonderful experience and for our beautiful little girl.

There was a lot to get done before we could return to Japan. A new government law required everyone to have their own passport, not simply be included in a parent's. So, at five days old, Noa had her first passport photo taken. It caused quite a few raised eyebrows down the track, when a three-year-old passed through immigration in several different countries looking nothing like the baby in the photo. Then, because she had her own passport, she also required a Japanese visa. It was a stupid rule that, as frequent travelers, cost us a lot of time and money at various foreign embassies.

Our last two weeks in Australia were spent mired down in paperwork and flight arrangements. Though it was sad for our families that we were saying goodbye yet again, and taking another grandchild away from them, I truly believed that it wouldn't be long before we were back for good. I'd fallen in love with the far north coast of New South Wales and thought we could make a life there amid friends and like-minded people. We were hippies at heart, and the easygoing atmosphere suited our lifestyle.

But we had a long way to go before that return would become a reality. And though I had no clue at the time, it would be under vastly different conditions to the scenario I had dreamed of the day we returned to Japan.

~

1991

51

HOME SWEET MATSUDO

Coming home to Japan after Noa's birth was a welcome but lonely prospect. Once the initial buzz of bringing a new baby to a foreign culture wore off, and once my housewife students had all been introduced to her, we fell into a comfortable daily routine. It still included almost daily trips to Matsudo to share lunch hours with James, though it was rather more difficult to get everyone and everything to and fro on one bicycle.

Initially, I was able to ride around with Mani on the rear bike seat and Noa safely ensconced in her carrier attached to my chest. I'd often seen Japanese mothers bearing similar burdens, so I knew it was possible. The bike was quite heavy, but I quickly got used to the balancing act required to remain upright. It definitely became more difficult if I happened to buy more groceries than Mani was able to hang on to.

Once she was big enough, I was able to load Noa into a front-fitting baby seat that attached to the handlebars. That took the pressure off my shoulders, but it meant that my legs were forced to pedal at an unusual angle because of the seat basket between my knees. I was certain I was going to have permanent issues with my gait due to the damage I was doing to my knees with every new journey to the shops.

Eventually, we found a Mani-sized bike, and when he had learned to ride well enough, he was able to graduate from my rear seat to his own pedal-powered machine.

In the early days of having two children, I frequently hung out in the toy sections of the local department stores. In a welcome nod to the constant demands of motherhood, larger Japanese stores provided baby feeding and change rooms on the same floor that housed children's clothing and toys. They were also generous with access to toy samples, providing a cordoned off area where kids could play with the demo models to their hearts' content while their mums tended to babies and toddlers in the mothers' room. They also provided a rooftop play area littered with coin-operated rides. It was Japanese convenience at its blissful best.

I didn't have many friends in Japan, Japanese or *gaijin*. James and I were both busy and wrapped up in our own little family world. We had naturally evolved that way and it was an easy symbiosis. However, one afternoon I noticed a foreigner at the other end of the baby change room in the department store. I normally wouldn't have given her a second glance, except this woman was also breastfeeding a baby girl, one that looked about the same age as Noa. We made eye contact briefly and smiled at each other nervously. But without a word, we both left the room.

For some reason, as I wandered around the department store following our brief encounter, I found myself looking for her. I wanted to run into her again, ask her about her daughter, whether she was born in Japan, where she was from, where she lived, what she was doing in Japan, how long she'd been here, information I'd never considered essential from casual acquaintances. Yet here I was seeking her company, wondering about her. I felt like I needed to talk to her.

I guess it was meant to be, because we did meet again that afternoon, and this time we spoke."How old is your daughter?" I blurted, skipping over the introduction pleasantries.

"Three months. And yours?" As it turned out, her baby was born just three days before Noa, and she had been born at the same hospital where I had been taken when I had the miscarriage several years ago. And that was all it took. We became fast friends. We had just about everything in common, from our babies to our philosophies, to our love of music and writing.

Over the next few months, we grew closer. We were practically inseparable. While our husbands were at work, we spent time together. If we weren't at each other's homes, we could be found in the nearest park with the kids, talking about life, the universe, and everything and following up with long phone conversations punctuated by children's needs and demands. It was such a relief to finally find a kindred spirit, one with whom I had so much in common and so much to share. We debated the trials and treasures of life in Japan, celebrated the highs and commiserated with the lows of life in general, and shared intimate details of the good and bad in our relationships.

Sue and her daughter were our constant companions. Our place, her place, the park. We were like the five musketeers. Mani required constant supervision lest he became over-enthusiastic with the girls in his role-playing games. He loved to pretend he was captain of a pirate ship and they were his crew, never mind that they were not even one year old and didn't get it at all. He was six years old when Noa was born, so the age difference was both a blessing and a curse. He could be helpful one minute and dangerous the next. Life was full, to say the least.

When Sue left the country a couple of years later and flew home to Australia with her second child, I was so sad. My only other contact with the world outside our door was with my housewife students. While they were kind, generous, wonderful women, they weren't friends in the truest sense of the word. They weren't Sue. Their Japanese-ness, my foreign-ness, and our ongoing teacher-student relationship would forever prevent any real closeness no matter how much we admired each other. None of them would ever have considered leaving Japan and moving their family to a country where they knew no one, didn't speak the language, and didn't have any real job prospects. I'm sure they thought James and me just a little insane, but that also made us strangely intriguing.

By the time we left Japan after almost eight years, they had decided that I was 'Japanese from the neck down'. It was the best compliment I could have hoped for. It gave me hope that, in some small way, I had changed their perception of the world outside Japan. Perhaps, like me, they had come to realize we weren't so different, that 'outside person' was really an unfair moniker. I hoped that I had opened their eyes to other possibilities, a different philosophy, an alternative that they hadn't thought an option, or were denied because of their binding cultural norms. But their unwillingness to discuss anything on a deep and meaningful level meant I would never know.

52

JOURNAL

May 13

My latest challenge is learning to patchwork. Sewing was never my forte, but since living here I've become quite the seamstress. Baby clothes are so expensive that I've taken to making them from scratch, everything from bloomers and sweet little dresses for Noa, and loose shirts and loud, printed pants for Mani. James brought home a dining table on the back of his bike about a month ago, and we actually bought some chairs to go with it, nice pine ones. We've obviously been here too long. Not that long ago, we would never have made such an investment. They would have come from the gomi or we'd have had none. They're a bit hard to sit on for any length of time, so I have made a patchwork cushion for each of them.

Mani is doing well with his schoolwork. His uncle gave him a computer and that has helped to get him interested in writing and numbers. A week or so after we got back here, he was doing simple additions on paper, where before that he couldn't even write the numbers from one to ten. I showed him once and he was off. Now I set him pages of additions and subtractions thinking to get something done on my own, and he finishes them in five seconds flat. The computer throws up random problems for him too, but the trouble is, the first *five are ridiculously easy and if you get them all correct, it plunges into double figures. Up until the other day we hadn't used it for a while, so it was especially good for him to find the double figures no problem. Now we're dealing with adding double figures to double figures. He knows how to do it, but the resulting answers are too big a concept for him. This isn't included in the curriculum we're using but he was asking. That's what's so nice about learning at home. Your program can be flexible and geared to individual interests. You might say it's learner-friendly.*

I've been in contact with Australian Home Schoolers, a group based in Sydney that is trying to coordinate the local information and regulations currently in vogue. It seems it's no longer under the control of the Education Department, though you do have to register and apply for an exemption in New South Wales. There are currently 400 families doing it, or should I say not doing school, in New South Wales. From their journal, it seems to me that a lot of them have taken their kids out of school for religious reasons, as well as those that feel that they were quite capable of educating their preschoolers and nothing changed when they reached that magic school age.

We feel that we are educating ourselves as well as educating Mani. You can't imagine what you lose when you give someone else authority over your life when they don't deserve it. The education system, the medical system, even the government. I'm not advocating anarchy. These processes have their place, but I have more faith in people and their ability to be responsible than in systems or institutions that try rather pathetically to maintain order by imposing stricter and stricter rules and regulations.

Noa is growing so fast; she doesn't look at all like a three-month-old baby. She is so wise and aware. Sometimes I feel like a real klutz when I try to do something for her and it's not what she wants and she gives me a look like, "Oh brother!"

Sue often calls me up and asks me all kinds of questions. I told her I'm probably the last person to ask because I don't follow any book. I told her she should trust herself. She was going crazy trying to follow the advice of her Japanese friends.

"Do I have to do that?" she asked, referencing some well-meant but ridiculous-sounding advice she had been given.

"Totally up to you," was all I could offer.

She is in Australia for three months now and I miss her and our long telephone conversations terribly. We hit it off right from the start. We must have, because I don't usually give out my phone number on the first meeting.

53

SPOKESWOMAN

Now that I had a very small baby to consider, I was forced to rethink my trips out of the house on the bike. Taking my lead from the locals, I strapped her into the chest mounted baby carrier and left my six-year-old son to the rear child seat. Once I'd done the shopping and loaded up the handlebars with numerous bags and odd shaped packages, the whole experience became a bit more of an Evil Knievel stunt, but over time I became quite adept at the task. Until one day when disaster struck.

I have to go back a bit and explain about my choice of wardrobe for the trip. Since riding around the streets of Matsudo was about the only exercise I was able to get, I wasn't exactly getting back to my pre-pregnancy body shape. This seriously limited my wardrobe decisions and my outfit of choice had become a voluminous, three-tiered, gypsy style skirt with an elasticized waistband. I topped off this fashion extravaganza with a loose-fitting t-shirt. It was almost the only thing that fit me and was definitely the most comfortable. Not quite as good a choice to match my mode of transport — a bicycle with no chain guard.

One sunny Saturday afternoon, I decided it might be nice to get a couple of videos from the local video store. That might not sound very exciting, but for people who kept their TV in the cupboard due to a lack of appropriate English language viewing options, it was a big night in. The video store was only a few miles from our house, up a steep hill, across the main road, and down a fairly busy side street, just beyond my favorite local supermarket. I decided I'd also pick up some snacks and supplies, since I was going to have to pass the store anyway.

Since I never went anywhere without my bub, I strapped her into her carrier and set off. The hill was always a challenge and as usual, I made it about one-third of the way up before I had to dismount and push. We crossed the main road and headed off down the side street, which was narrow by western standards. We hadn't made it far along when it suddenly became hard to pedal, and I had to strain to make any progress. Then abruptly, all progress ceased, and the pedals refused to turn at all. I glanced behind me to see my skirt had become inextricably twisted around a couple of spokes in the rear wheel and was caught up in the links of the chain. When I tried to get off the bike, I was almost publicly disrobed by the tension between the chain and the skirt. I discovered that it was the right side of the skirt that had become trapped, so the only way I was able to move was to let go of the handlebars and physically turn in a clockwise direction until I was facing the way I had come. With Noa strapped to my chest, trying to disentangle the mess was beyond the realm of possibility.

As luck would have it, I could see a sign announcing '*Jitensha-ya*'[1] in large Japanese characters just 50 yards back down the road. However, my only option for retracing my steps to get there was to physically pick up the bike and carry it, backwards, until I reached the workshop. I can't imagine what the passing locals thought of this sight, but none of them offered to assist the crazy *gaijin*.

When I reached the shop, there was no one in sight, so in my best textbook Japanese, I called out for help. I had intended to say, "Could you please help me?" but later I discovered what I had actually said was, "Why don't you help me?" which was rather less polite, if not apt. The tiny old man who appeared from the shadows to rescue me was unperturbed at the spectacle of the crazy foreigner at his shop front anchored to a bicycle chain by her clothing. He was also pretty deft with a knife and quickly freed the entangled cloth without tearing it any more than it was already. There were, however, quite a few train track grease marks trailing across the bottom most layer of the skirt.

I thanked him profusely in perfect Japanese and asked him how much I owed him, also in perfect Japanese. I had long since mastered the delicate art of shopping dialogue. He refused to accept any money, content instead to retreat to the interior of his open fronted shop stifling laughter. Not to be put off by my unfortunate incident, I decided to resume my journey to the video store. Heck, I was quite close now.

The video store was set up in the same kind of layout as supermarket aisles with one major difference. So that the counter staff could keep an eye on their customers and preempt any kind of video concealment, there was a giant convex mirror positioned high above the shelves in the corner of the store. As I walked up and down making my selections, I happened to glance in the mirror's general direction and noticed that there was actually more damage to my skirt than I had at first thought. Appallingly, there was a large three-corner tear in the back that coincided perfectly with the point where my legs attached to my butt, right on the panty line. While in the store, I was protected by the high rows of shelving and relative lack of customers. So, I calmly paid for the videos and returned to my bike.

Making sure I wasn't going to incur another incident, I proceeded back towards the supermarket, still intent on purchasing the snacks and supplies that would accompany our night of viewing heaven. The supermarket was somewhat busier than the video store and the aisles wider, so in order to maintain a shred of decency and dignity, I was forced to walk around collecting items while holding the three-corner tear in my skirt closed. It worked a treat... until I reached the checkout.

In order to pay for the goods I had selected, I needed two hands, which meant temporarily releasing my grip on the rear of my skirt while I handed over the cash. Because I was now standing in a line, I enacted this maneuver as quickly as I could, grabbing the rear of my skirt again as I left the store. There was another convex mirror strategically placed at the store entrance and when I spied my own image walking towards my bike, I could see that I had not quite grabbed hold of the right location on the skirt. I was, in fact, holding the three-corner tear open instead of closed, thereby exposing myself to everyone who had the misfortune to be walking behind me. My face turned the color of overripe strawberries.

When we lived in the *gaijin* house, we used to joke about what the Japanese might have thought of the foreigners living in their midst. The general consensus was that it was probably something like *bakka gaijin* in crumpled clothes. I'm sure my little skirt episode did nothing to dispel this myth and everything to inflame it.

I did repair my favorite skirt by removing the bottom most layer, cutting out the grease-stained and torn sections and piecing it all back together. I even wore it again while riding the bike. And, yes, it did get caught again, not far from home. The friendly farmer who disentangled me that time was not as skilled with a knife and though he apologized profusely, he simply sliced out an entire section. He did try to pull it free first but, in the end, I exhorted him to cut the wretched thing. Anything, just get me out of this mess. This made further repairs untenable, and I had to bin it.

I bought another skirt not long after the demise of my favorite purple one. It was very similar to the one I lost in the entanglement fiasco, so whenever I wore it out on the bike, I had to hold it bunched up together in my spare hand while I rode. Spare hand. Now there's a joke. I was riding a bike, holding my skirt together, balancing at least three bags of groceries on the handlebars, toting a day pack, and a baby in a front-loading baby seat. What the hell was a spare hand? Maybe I should have invested in roof racks. It couldn't have looked any more ridiculous.

54
CAN I BORROW YOUR WASHING MACHINE?

The physical isolation of our house in the cabbage fields meant it was rare that anyone knocked at our door, and if they did, they didn't make the same mistake twice. The challenge of explaining to the resident *gaijin* what they actually wanted was a huge deterrent. I had turned away many traveling kimono salesmen, hawkers of Japanese snacks, even passersby asking for directions with a simple *Wakarimasen!* Though I understood quite a lot of Japanese, I was often guilty of taking the easy way out rather than allowing the conversation to degenerate into an extended exchange of *"Ah so desu ka?"*[1] as I answered the inevitable questions about where we were from, how long we'd been in Japan, and how I liked it.

Despite the fact that the little lane way that ran past the front of our house was a badly maintained strip of bitumen, it was still well used. In the rainy season it was often impassable, especially when heavy rain had washed most of the soil from the fields onto the road surface. In their infinite wisdom, the Matsudo City Council chose a particularly wet summer to dig up and resurface the roadway. Work progress had come to a complete stop and the mud outside our front door had turned to an ankle-deep quagmire unfit for any form of transport. The school kids had worked this out the hard way and were using an alternate parallel route a couple of blocks north of our house. But an unsuspecting tennis aficionado on a motor scooter had unwittingly fallen victim to the sticky mess. She had come off the bike in the worst possible spot for both of us – the thickest mud, and right outside the *gaijin* house.

She stood in my doorway dressed from top to toe in what must once have been tennis whites. But now they were far from white, splattered all over in thick, dark mud. It wasn't hard to guess what had happened.

"*Ohayo gozaimasu.*[2] *Watashi*... lots of unintelligible Japanese words... *sentaki*... more words I didn't understand... *arimasu ka?*" It was pretty obvious that the poor woman needed to change and wash up. But what she had said caught me by surprise. Somewhere in her quickly spoken sentences, I'm sure I heard the word *sentaki*.[3] She wanted to use my washing machine?

She began to remove her shoes in my *genkan* as if I had already agreed to her request. In truth, I was the one in shock and my face must have reflected that. But she was busily preparing to come inside and didn't notice. So, not wishing to appear unnerved and unsympathetic, I quickly ushered her inside and in the direction of our bathroom, which was conveniently located just inside the front door. Though this had seemed unusual when we moved in, it now took on a more fortuitous quirk.

She disappeared inside and shut the door, leaving me out in the hallway wondering whether I had removed the towels from the floor after our morning ablutions, refilled the deep tub with fresh water, replaced the cover on the squat toilet, and how long it may have been since I had cleaned the urinal. Oh my God, it may have been a complete disaster in there. Just as I was turning every shade of embarrassment, she stuck her head outside the door and asked for a towel. I jumped, jolted into action by the shame of being caught loitering creepily in the hallway. Then she handed me all the once-white clothes she had been wearing. I assumed, more than a little incredulously, that these were meant to go in the washing machine she had asked to borrow. I felt like I was caught in some dreadful reality show scenario. Surprise! You're on candid camera! Certainly, no one was going to believe me when I retold this story.

Now, the Japanese are technologically advanced. Just one trip to the electronic center of the world, Akihabara in central Tokyo, is enough to confirm that. But even in the early 1990s, washing machines were not their forte. If you were lucky enough to actually have enough space in your 2LDK *apato* (a 2-room apartment with a combined lounge/dining/kitchen), you undoubtedly had a twin tub machine, not a top-loading automatic. They still did the job, but it was a slow process. And it was especially slow in our little house because I had to connect the outdoor hose to the garden tap in order to fill it up. Cold water was the only option. It stood precariously on the tiny veranda outside our second bedroom. Yes, that's right. Outside.

My visitor was lucky she hadn't turned up at my door the week before. Back then, I didn't even have a washing machine and had washed all our clothes in the bathroom by hand. Tedious and time-consuming to say the least. When my Ichikawa housewife group discovered this fun fact, they quickly found me a near-new twin tub from among their ranks which I accepted most gratefully. I hadn't used one of these old-fashioned machines in years and doing so now felt a bit like returning to the days of the old mangle. But it was far better than the one I didn't have.

Though I was still learning how to decipher the mess of Japanese symbols that defined the button functions, I knew one thing for sure — the quickest cycle took about an hour to complete and still involved manually transferring the clothes from tub to spinner. The cold water did little more than move mud around inside the tub for most of that time, after which I switched the three stained items of clothing over to the spinner. They came out damp and dirty, almost the same way they had gone in. I had no dryer, so I couldn't help her out further.

During the whole laborious process, she sat in my lounge room on a chair only recently retrieved from the *gomi*, drinking coffee from a cup also rescued on a midnight raid, but scared of engaging me in any further conversation. Maybe she recognized the cup or the furniture as something she herself had recently discarded. The awkward silence was a tense time for both of us. I busied myself cleaning up the kitchen sink several times over. Mani tried to show her all his Lego, and any other toy he could find. She smiled at him, tittered appropriately at Noa in the universal language unique to babies and toddlers, and gripped the coffee cup so tightly I thought it might break.

Before she left, she tried to pay me a couple of thousand yen. I politely refused and sent her on her way, watching her disappear hesitantly down the muddy track on her scooter. It took me a while to recover from the unexpected start to the day, but I could only imagine the story she told when she finally caught up with her tennis buddies. I always wondered if it was a tale about this weird *gaijin* who made her wait while I washed her clothes, when all she wanted was to wash up and get changed.

JOURNAL

July 24

I'm writing this entry at 12:30 a.m. because it's the only time of day when I don't feel like a baked vegetable. We took James' lunch up to him at 3 o'clock this afternoon and nearly fried our brains. Noa got a touch of color. It's miserable. I sat on top of the fan most of the day and still sweated buckets. We turned on the air con unit for the first time in four years yesterday but after it blew four years of dust out the vent and seemed to be working, we discovered the fan on the unit outside wasn't turning. I don't know if it's supposed to turn or not, but I'd hate to see the front wall of the house blown out, as much as we could use the space. So, we turned it off again. Who knows what might have crawled inside in the last four years.

We are having our share of battles with the summer vermin again. We rid the kitchen of fruit fly only to be overrun by cockroaches. The mouse in the wall seems to have given up biting at the screw hole above the spice rack, but something is definitely on the move in the ceiling in the front room.

The story of the skirt caught in the bicycle wheel has an unfortunate sequel. Yes, it happened again. This time just around the corner from home, but still too far to carry the bike home backwards. I was about to send Mani home for a pair of scissors when a field man came walking around the corner with a very *sharp knife. He tried to pull it out first, but in the end I told him to cut the wretched thing just to get me free. He apologized profusely and I bowed and gomen nasai'ed all over the place and went home to squeeze into the only pair of jeans I have that still fit me. I'm still trying to work out how I can reattach all the pieces of the skirt; maybe I could turn it into a patchwork skirt. Or here's a thought: wear some more appropriate riding gear.*

1992

JOURNAL

February 12

Mother Nature has certainly been kicking Tokyo around this month. First we had the heaviest snowfall in 30 years and a day later, a rock 'n' roll earthquake of equal magnitude to the one we suffered through when we lived in Shimoyagiri. It hit us early in the morning and caused a real racket. Nothing broke at our place, but a wall in Molly's kitchen cracked and plaster fell off. Our houses are about the same vintage.

The previous day's snow had brought down the power and telephone lines. Because we had no power, the pump on the well couldn't operate, so we also had no water. But, thankfully, we have a gas stove and there was plenty of snow at the front door to scoop up and make into tea. I had to be careful not to dig too deep else I ended up with mud as well.

They fixed the power by early afternoon, but we had to wait a couple of days for the phone. When they finally reconnected us, they got it back to front and we had the Ito's number and vice versa. Relatives had been trying to call us since the earthquake, which had actually made the news in Australia. They got through while the second batch of linesmen were still here. Five minutes earlier and they'd have been talking to one of the Ito-san's, or trying to. We had a small after-shock a day later at about seven in the morning. The radio reported it was centered in approximately the same place under Tokyo Bay. I'm glad they don't happen so often, and that we will be away from it for a while, since we've decided to take another offshore break.

We're finally going back to Nepal after almost four years. We'll spend a month there, probably do a trek, and then have two weeks in Thailand on the way back. We'll do the beach thing somewhere in the south, maybe Phi Phi. We haven't been over that side of Thailand in forever. We leave in just over a week on Air India to Bangkok, then on to Kathmandu. We'll be back in early April.

I guess one day we may just pick up and leave here. We've been in this house for five years, the longest I've lived anywhere since I left home. Though we came to live in Japan as a way to finance our travels, it's become so much more than that. It's come to feel like home, so much so that it's hard to think of living somewhere else, even though we could never be truly accepted here. How strange that I could feel this way in a place where, at times, I feel so isolated.

57

DECISION

*L*eaving the country with two kids in tow was more challenging than our previous travels, but it didn't deter us. The drive to prove it could be done was strong. Despite our misgivings, Air India delivered us safely into Bangkok and Royal Nepal conveyed us to our beloved Kathmandu.

With only six weeks in which to get everything done that we had planned, we had to move fast on the trekking permits and gear hire. So, within a week of arriving in the Kingdom, we had everything arranged, and had set off on another trek in the direction of Everest Base Camp. This adventure is detailed in my first book, *Restless*, so I won't repeat it here. Suffice to say we didn't manage to get all the way to Base Camp, but we did rise to the challenge of walking the high Himalayan trails for over two weeks with two young children.

When we returned to Kathmandu, we slipped easily back into our daily habit of coffee and cake in the little tea shop in Thamel still run by our friend, Sanu. Trapped in this dead-end job for years now, and more than a little determined to better himself, Sanu began to enquire about the possibility of us taking him to Japan for work. With each day that passed, his pleas became more insistent, but we had only recently been granted full working visas ourselves and were in no position to sponsor anyone else to visit the country even as a tourist, let alone to work. If he managed to get into Japan at all, he would have to work illegally.

Being the perceptive young man that he was, Sanu changed his approach to focus on me; he knew I was more sympathetic to his cause. He begged me to convince James to allow him to come to Japan, as if that were his biggest obstacle. I held little hope of him being granted any kind of visa, but without our help his application was likely doomed. So, I began to argue his side. He deserved a break. What harm could there be in trying?

In the end, James agreed. Together we drafted a letter of support offering him accommodation and financial assistance during his visit. Blindly, and perhaps naively, we hoped it might convince the Japanese Embassy officials to grant him a short-term tourist visa. And to our great surprise, it worked. Sanu was overjoyed. By the time we left Nepal, he had booked and paid for his ticket to Tokyo, and we had agreed to meet him at the airport when he arrived.

On the way back to Japan, we passed through Thailand again. We had been there so often it had almost become our second home and we counted one local family as lifelong friends. But this time we needed a beach, a quiet, relaxing beach, a beach where we could regroup and recover before returning to the urban sprawl and teeming urbanity of Tokyo. The universe responded to our needs and brought us to Koh Phangan and the stunning Bottle Beach.

I'm not sure where we heard about this hidden gem or how we managed to find the long-tail boat that ferried us there from the tiny outpost of Chaloklum on the island's north shore, but it was a rare and lucky find. Just two sets of bungalows graced the shoreline, keeping their distance from each other by occupying either end of the beach. We chose the one directly in front of the landing site.

The Swiss guy behind the desk in the open-air restaurant greeted us warmly and directed us to one of the bungalows just back from the beach, in the second row. It was basic but adequate and it wasn't long before the kids had donned their swimsuits and were in the water, while we drank smoothies and watched on from the tables at the front of the restaurant. It was perfect — peaceful, beautiful, laid back, off the beaten track. The only access was by long-tail boat or long walk, so it was isolated from the tourist crowds. And it was cheap. We ate and drank like royalty on a pauper's budget. After an entire week, the four of us had spent less than ¥10,000 ($100).

But a week was nowhere near long enough in paradise; it was only long enough to know that we must return one day. We just didn't know how soon that would be.

JOURNAL

April 27

We've been back a month already and life is still not back to normal, thank goodness! Normal can be very humdrum some days. I'm addicted to change, I guess. Having family arrive for a visit only two days after we got home has kept up the pace, but now we're looking at our dwindling bank account and thinking we need a massive injection of funds as James is fond of saying.

While James' sister was here, we hired a car for a few days and drove down to Kyoto. We had planned to venture further afield but time wasn't on our side, and the urge to shop was strong in our guest, to the point where an infuriated Mani exclaimed, "You only came here to shop. You're just like Nanna!" Mani hates shopping. And he had high expectations based on her performance in Byron last year, which was pretty hard to beat. Back then, she had been his biggest and best playmate. He's learning an important lesson about space — other people's that is – and that things don't always stay the same.

Speaking of space, short-term visitors have a difficult time in the crowds here. They are used to having so much that crowded shops, trains, and streets full of people encroach just a bit too much. Still, we found lots of less stressful ways to fill the time and still managed not to do everything we all wanted to do.

Breaking news. I am now a published writer. Some time ago, I turned one of our amusing travel adventures into an article and submitted it to the editor of The Japan Times. My story ran while we were away. I received ¥2,000 for it (1200 words), but the biggest thrill was the byline. I hope to publish lots more in the future and work has resumed in earnest on my book. I was surprised to receive the check because it had been so long since I submitted the article that I'd forgotten all about it. Four months from submission to publication and five months to payment. I have no idea if that's standard.

The other noteworthy item is that we have bought a car. That sounds really permanent, but it isn't necessarily. It's a seller's market here. The gentleman we bought it from got 15 calls about it. Last week, I got all the way to a station on the other side of Tokyo to keep an appointment to look at another car, only to find it had been sold out from under me.

We don't actually have the car yet, only the parking space. It's only been driven around town in the last few years, so it probably needs the cobwebs blown out. It has registration until March 1993 and insurance until May. We plan to use it to get out of town on the weekends, if we can brave the weekend traffic. At least they drive on the same side of the road as we do back home. We just need to learn a few more kanji so that we can read the road signs.

It looks like our first major expedition in the car will be out to the airport to collect Sanu. He arrives in a couple of weeks and is coming to stay with us, as we agreed in Nepal. I've made some enquiries with my housewife groups and they've promised to ask around their friends to see if anyone could use an enterprising young man's help in a paid capacity. It's a long shot but I've no idea how else to help him get work without a proper visa. Getting him into the country is only the beginning.

59

THE EXPAT CAR SHUFFLE

*T*aking a break from Japan this last time had done nothing to settle our nomad spirits or soothe our itchy feet. We wanted to keep going, keep moving, not just come back and continue in the same boring routine. Since we couldn't afford to leave again so soon, the next best solution was to see some more of Japan.

We had already found lots of interesting nooks and crannies that would have remained a blur from the seat of a car. But getting further afield and off the beaten track required transportation of a more individual nature. It also made more sense now that there were four of us.

"What if we bought a car?" I suggested late one evening. The kids were finally asleep, and I was taking a private 'me' moment to flip through the latest issue of *Tokyo Journal*. Expats often advertised all manner of belongings in the local magazine when they were about to leave the country and return home.

"How much would that cost?" James seemed open to the idea.

"Not as much as you might think. There are a couple listed in here for around the ¥60,000 mark, but a few more at around ¥100,000. That's less than $1,000 on average." I was pleasantly surprised by what I saw.

"Might not get much of a car for that price."

"Doesn't hurt to check them out, though. Want me to make some calls?"

"Sure. Why not?" So, we agreed to at least look into the process.

Though the purchase took place towards the end of our eight-year stay when the language barrier was diminished, it wasn't easy. The process was a nightmare, designed to confuse and confound even the best prepared foreigner. Just beating out everyone else in the *gaijin* community to view the vehicle was a feat in itself. When we answered our fifth advert minutes after it was posted on a local community bulletin board, we weren't even first. In fact, it had already been sold. But the vendor took a liking to us, or more likely to our blonde-haired kids, and graciously agreed to sell it out from under the winning bidder for a slightly higher offer.

We bought a Datsun Sunny California station wagon. Where do they come up with these names? It only had 25,000 kms on it even though it was 12 years old. My housewife students couldn't believe that we had bought such an old car, since they routinely scrapped their own after only two years. A 12-year-old car was clearly ten years past its use by date. The previous owner was in her 80s and hadn't driven for years. When it had been out of the garage, it only went around town, to the shops and back, though why you would go to the trouble of getting the car out for that caper was beyond me. Needless to say, it had a few cobwebs that needed displacing.

We learned the hard way that there were lots of rules around owning a car in Japan, not least of which was having somewhere to park it at night. In fact, unless you had a piece of paper that proved you had somewhere to park it, you couldn't even get the vehicle registered. We were knee-deep in paperwork for weeks trying to get it all together — proof of this, proof of that, and at each turn a catch-22. You had to have one before you could get the other, but to get the other you had to have the first one. And it wasn't cheap, either. Check out the figures:

Cost of vehicle — ¥95,000 (about $1,000 at the time)

Cost of registration — ¥45,000

Cost of insurance — ¥40,000

Cost of parking space — ¥10,000 per month, in other words, more than the car for a year's worth of parking.

The other annoying thing about our car space, beside the expense, was its proximity to our house, or rather, lack of proximity. We had to ride our bikes about ten minutes up the road to reach it. Hardly convenient. Especially when it rained. On those days, I took to parking just down the road underneath the giant electrical tower. It was illegal, but I figured we were so isolated that no one would ever notice. But no.

Just a week out from our departure from Japan, I pulled up underneath the tower for what would be the last time. We'd given up the parking space rather than pay another month's rent, so I had no other option. As I was gathering the kids and the groceries, a young police officer dismounted his bicycle beside the driver's side window and bid me good day. The conversation that ensued took place entirely in Japanese.

"Do you own this car?" He was young, and not the least put off by my foreign face.

I wanted to retort sarcastically, *"No I just found it unlocked with the keys inside and decided to take it for a spin."* But instead I replied in my most polite Japanese, "Yes, of course, officer."

"Do you have a parking space?" Not surprisingly, he knew the rules.

I wanted to argue the injustice of having spent the last year paying through the nose for a parking space that was neither cheap nor convenient, and now that I had only one week left in the country, he objected to me parking under this tower.

But instead I said, "Until last week I had a parking space just a little way up the road. But we are leaving Japan next week and we canceled it. Would it be a problem if I parked here for just a few more days?"

"I'm very sorry but I cannot allow it. It's the law that you must have off-street parking for your vehicle. You will have to move it today." His demeanor was sympathetic, but his words were unrelenting.

For some reason, this annoyed me more than it should have. I guess I was tired of towing the line. Easy things had become obstacles; and obstacles had become irritating. The timing was right for me to leave the country I had called home for several years.

My head screamed, *"You miserable bastard. I have unquestioningly obeyed every stupid rule you have in this country, from fingerprinting to copious gift giving, apologizing for just about everything, carrying an Alien Registration card at ALL times, and now with just one week to go before I leave, you want to penalize me for not doing the right thing?"* The irony of it. Clearly, I was ready to leave Japan.

But instead I said, "Please forgive me. I will move it as soon as I drop off my groceries at home, which is just down the road there. I'm sorry I have inconvenienced you." And I pointed towards our house, just 50 yards away, and bowed as deeply as I could from the driver's seat of the car.

"Thank you very much." His job done, he got back on his bike, and as he rode away, I made a mental note to continue with my civil disobedience. I didn't have a lot of choice. We had no parking space. And anyway, what was the worst he could do? Deport me?

JOURNAL

July 12

Today Mani's new friend, Yoshihiro, called up and asked us to go to a fete in the park near their house. The kids had a ball. Afterwards we all went out to a noodle shop for dinner — four adults and four kids. Yoshihiro ate two meals and dessert. He's nine, but Mani is as big as him. It's nice that he's not afraid of Mani and not bothered by any language problem. He gets his message across somehow.

The house is a bit of a farm again this summer. Mice, cockroaches, flies, ants, mosquitoes. About the only thing we don't have, YET, is fruit fly, and that's only because it's been so cold. Beginning of July and we're still sleeping under the winter futon. Hopefully the rainy season is over now and the lake at the front door will dry up. The poor cabbages must be sick to death of being sprayed with mud each time a car passes. The problem was exacerbated by the fact that just before the rainy season began, they decided to dump tons of dredged up sludge on the three fields that surround our house to build them up. It didn't stay long where they dumped it and now most of it is on the roadway — hence the lake.

We've been getting out and about in the car. Yesterday we went over to Kujukuri Beach on the Pacific coast in Chiba Prefecture, and last week to a *train park on the other side of Tokyo. The weekend before that we drove down to Yokohama and over the new Bay Bridge. I thought it was just a local joke, but young couples really do park up there, right in the left-hand lane. You'd think it would get boring, listening to the constant banter from the loudspeakers — "Please do not stop!" — but I imagine they're not there to listen to that. There are many occasions in Japan when a public address system is used; earthquake and pollution warnings spring to mind. Perhaps no one is listening to any of it anymore. I did notice how easy it would be to jump from the top of the bridge since there are no high fences offering a deterrent.*

I ended up having to drive back across Tokyo at 9 p.m. that night, which was almost as suicidal as the bridge jumping idea. All because of one wrong turn. Shinjuku was just a blur of neon and taxi horns, as was Ueno. What a nightmare. I was glad I knew vaguely where each signposted destination was, or we may have ended up God knows where. In fact, I think we did, but it turned out to be close to Matsudo. If there is an unfortunate next time, I'll stick to the elevated freeway, which is marginally less stressful. I think I've finally gotten used to the narrowness of the streets, a very loose term in some cases.

Mani's new math course arrived yesterday. It's brilliant. I wish someone had taught me these tricks 25 years ago. We are still waiting on his new computer — GeoSafari — a geography-oriented course. He's just about completed a course on volcanology for gifted kindergarteners to grade threes. The final project was building a plaster of Paris replica and watching it erupt by mixing bi-carb soda and vinegar. This went well with our recent science project on acid-base reactions. He is very interested in science, and very keen on learning to read and is working hard on that. The problem is that he is terribly bored by all those simplistic readers, so we have to work our way through simplified versions of Journey to the Centre of the Earth etc. We read; he follows.

Learning with him is so exciting. I feel like I'm getting an education all over again, one that is based on interest and ability or appropriateness rather than dates, names, and unrelated facts I learned just to be first on my feet in tests and classroom competitions. I don't remember much about any of it now, much less use it. And all those A's and first in class results didn't get me a degree or a good job. I think I've had to unlearn much more.

I wish I'd known what I really wanted to do when I left high school. There were so many options, but it came down to Sydney Uni and a degree in Pharmacy, or Newcastle Uni and a teachers' scholarship. The scholarship won simply because it meant I could be closer to home, and to James. Looking back, I see now that I based one of the major decisions of my life on such arbitrary criteria. School never prepared me for that decision, or any other for that matter.

I think I'm ready to leave Japan. I'm tired, tired of feeling isolated, tired of struggling with 'We Japanese.' I'm tired of being a gaijin. It's time to get off the merry-go-round, to go home for a while and catch up with me. As much as I've enjoyed our time in Japan, I feel as though I've put part of my life, myself, on hold while we've been here. You can do everything you need to do here, but not everything you want to do.

James will never agree to go back to Australia. He's not ready. I'm not sure he ever will be ready, and I'm not sure why he resists the idea so strongly. He has made his feelings quite clear on many occasions. The best I can hope for is that he will agree to go somewhere else.

But it's time to raise the issue.

1993

61

THE FINAL CHAPTER

After our last visit to Nepal and Thailand, I found it hard to settle back into Japan. The stopover in Thailand on the way home had disturbed me, awakened me to the humdrum of the life we were living. I had tired of the constant commuting and teaching, racing headlong towards the end of another year in Japan without being any closer to moving on. A few weeks on the beaches of Koh Phangan almost a year ago had made me yearn for a quiet life, relaxing under palm trees and bathing in warm blue seas. Though that was far from the reality of bungalow life, the concept was extremely alluring.

I sensed that James felt it too. He was distant and distracted by things going on at the school, things that I wasn't part of or privy to. We were drifting, and not in a good way, not the way we once had when just a few years earlier we had wandered footloose across the globe. We were also drifting apart, and with no other close friends in our lives, we were losing the anchor that was our relationship. Either something was going to snap under the strain, or we were. In my mind, we had reached the turning point, and I hoped that a new environment might breathe life back into our tired reality.

"Do you think it might be time to leave Japan?" I'm not sure now which one of us asked the question that had filled the room like an elephant. But once it was out there, we could deal with it.

"Where would we go? I'm not going back to Australia." James was always adamant that he didn't want to go home. It clearly wasn't on the table.

"How about Thailand then. Maybe we could finally get that business off the ground." We had made a couple of feeble attempts to become drop-ship entrepreneurs and free ourselves from the drudgery of our nine-to-five lives, but get rich quick schemes were never going to be the answer. "I could do my writing. Maybe I could make some money from that, enough to save us from having to dip into our savings. Those bungalows we found on Koh Phangan would be a wonderful place for the kids, for all of us. And they were cheap."

"Yeah, it was a find, that's for sure." At least we agreed on that.

So, without much more discussion, we began to make the moves that would take us away from our home of the last eight years and on to our next adventure. That prospect alone was enough to lift our spirits, renew the purpose in our lives.

There was a lot to do. We had to sell the car, the telephone shares, the electronic piano. Those were our most valuable possessions and highly sought after by other *gaijin*. The rest had come from the *gomi* and could mostly go back there, unless we could palm them off to another new arrival in the country.

We had to decide what was going to travel with us and what we could send on ahead without too much expense. There were some hard decisions to make. We had to part with some much-loved treasures. Even if they had been rescued from the *gomi*, they had been part of our lives for most of our time in Japan.

Sanu came over to help us pack up. My housewife friends had come through for us yet again and found him a job within a couple of weeks of his arrival. He had been working in a neighboring suburb as a jeweler's assistant ever since. They had even provided him free accommodation on site. He lived frugally, sending some of the money he earned back to his family in Nepal and saving as much as he could. I could tell it was hard for him to watch us pack. He couldn't bear to see so many useful items disposed of and kept suggesting I reconsider some of my discard decisions.

"Either you take it, Sanu, or it's going in the rubbish." That became my chant as I waded through all our possessions, from the rice cooker to the kitchen scales and our dependable bicycles. He claimed what he could, but in the end resigned himself to watching me cram perfectly serviceable items into endless garbage bags. Even after I posted off 180 pounds of books, toys, and clothes to Thailand in four large boxes, Sanu left the house with almost as much luggage as we did.

The Ito's were shocked that we were leaving and seemed to genuinely wish we weren't. We had been good tenants, never made too much noise, and always paid the rent. We went away for long periods on vacations they never understood, but we had always come back. On the day we left the house, all four of them lined up in the driveway to say *sayonara*.[1] Ito-san the Mr. bowed deeply and handed James a wad of cash.

"*Reikin o henkin shimasu, yo.*" He was returning some of our key money, the money we had paid as a thank you each time we had renewed our lease — two years' worth, about ¥80,000. It was unheard of, but a measure of our mutual respect. We also bowed deeply in return and thanked them all profusely. Though I felt like we hardly knew them, it was an emotional leave-taking.

We still had another 200 pounds of luggage to struggle with, 50 pounds for each of us, kids included since we had purchased seats for them both. We had to use the farm trolley that had served us so well on our late night *gomi* raids to get it all up to the bus stop at the top of the hill. And it was no mean feat to get it on and off the talking bus and then the airport Skyliner train. But somehow, we managed. I have no idea what happened to the farm trolley, except that it never got onto the bus with us. It may well have sat there on the side of the highway, abandoned, a solitary *gaijin* relic of eight years in Japan.

We spent our last couple of hours in Japan unceremoniously scoffing sushi in one of the airport restaurants. Even the lowly airport fare was far superior to any Japanese dishes we were going to get in the foreseeable future. We ate and ate, uncaring of the cost. Everyone was quiet until the last plate was empty and we couldn't fit in even one more grain of rice.

An hour later we were bound for Bangkok. The six-and-a-half-hour flight was a welcome respite from the rigors of dragging all our luggage on and off various forms of domestic transport. The kids were excited to be heading to a beach; they didn't understand that we still had many buses, trains, and ferries to negotiate before we finally arrived.

But the end was in sight. We were at the beginning of the end. Yet none of us realized how accurately that sentence would define our lives on a remote Thai beach in the coming months.

NOTES

1. Time Out

1. An austere Buddhist meditation technique based on breathing.

2. Are We Japanese or Are We Aliens?

1. Japanese term for peace and harmony. Upsetting the communal wa by behaving badly or selfishly is particularly frowned upon. By not graciously accepting the responses of the innkeepers, I had forced them to be rude to me.

3. One Door Closes...

1. Colloquial term for non-Japanese or foreigner, having been shortened from the more formal gai-koku-jin. The literal translation of gaijin is outside person.
2. A traditional Japanese style inn.

4. The Talking Bus

1. A major Japanese department store chain with a supermarket on the first floor.
2. Another Japanese supermarket chain with a large bakery section on the first floor.
3. Skylark – a popular Japanese/western restaurant chain.
4. Characters in the Japanese writing system that were originally borrowed from Chinese.

5. Gaijin House

1. Very overused term for cute, often heard in long, high-pitched tones by hordes of young Japanese girls.
2. A one on one platonic date. The hostesses were expected to meet a client for dinner once a week or so and then bring them to the club afterwards.
3. A slang term for crazy, stupid, a fool. We often referred to ourselves as *bakka gaijin* – crazy foreigners.

6. Journal

1. Cute, as described above.

7. House Rules

1. Traditional straw and reed mats about 3 feet by 6 feet in size, edged in brocade, and arranged in standard room sizes of 4 1/2, 6, 8 and 12 mats.
2. The entrance to any Japanese dwelling, typically one step below the level of the main floor, where shoes are removed and stored before entering the home.
3. Japanese term for rubbish of all kinds, from kitchen waste to unwanted household items.
4. Used as an apology, I'm sorry, or excuse me in just about any situation.
5. Small cylinder engraved on one end with the owner's name in Japanese characters. Used as a signature on all official documents.

9. Getting Hired

1. Scramble crossing – a pedestrian crossing where all traffic stops and pedestrians may cross in all directions at once, including diagonally.

11. A Yen for Savings

1. The discarded crusts from either end of a loaf of bread, sold in huge bags for ¥20 and sometimes given away for free.
2. "I'm a vegetarian."
3. "Is that right?" Very handy exclamation to know that covers a myriad responses to almost anything.
4. Pickled radish.
5. A kind of vegetable.
6. A concoction of fermented soybeans with a very nasty smell and very acquired taste.
7. Cucumber pickled when used in sushi rolls.
8. Pickled plum mixed with chopped perilla leaves.
9. Ya is the suffix used to denote a shop. So, a *tofu-ya* is a shop that sells tofu.
10. A concoction of fermented soybeans with a very nasty smell and very acquired taste.
11. "Really?" or "True?" used as an expression of disbelief.

12. House Hunter

1. "I'm so sorry" or "Excuse me."
2. Japanese rendition of the English word 'present'.

14. Home Visit

1. A long, wooden instrument with 13 strings often played by geisha at a tea ceremony or to entertain guests.
2. Commonly used, informal word for please.

3. Official term for Japanese Tea Ceremony

18. The Cycling Real Estate Agent

1. One of Japan's alphabets used to spell out the endings of the Japanese words that the Chinese characters can't allow for. The other alphabet is *katakana*, used to spell out foreign words phonetically.
2. "How interesting."
3. Japanese for yes.
4. Slang term for "Amazing!" or Wow!" Yo is used for emphasis at the end of a statement.

20. Moving Day

1. "I'm sorry!" or "I apologize."
2. There is no distinction in the Japanese honorific naming system between men and women that corresponds to the English titles of Mr. and Mrs. The postnominal use of *san* is attributed to both, which makes it difficult to distinguish between the landlord and his wife in this text. Hence, my arbitrary addition of -the Mr. and -the Mrs. after their names.

21. The Gaijin Next Door

1. Literally as it sounds – gas range.
2. "This is great isn't it?"
3. Thank you very much, polite version.
4. Spring onions or green onions.
5. Familiar term for older brother.

25. Kyoto by Trains

1. Mt Fuji is usually referred to as Fujisan in Japanese, but rather than being an honorific suffix as used with proper names, 'san' is one pronunciation of the character for mountain.
2. Don't have any of…
3. Railway station.
4. From.

26. Christmas in Kyoto

1. An honorific term for aunt or older woman.
2. A simple, Japanese house coat, much like a short form of the *kimono*.
3. Traditional deep Japanese bath filled with hot water for soaking in after washing.

4. Japanese hot spring, often outdoor, but also used to describe a hotel or *ryokan* using spring water in its shared bathrooms.
5. Japanese bedding. You sleep on a thick, firm futon and under another lighter one called a *kakebuton*. The whole ensemble is simply referred to as *futon*.
6. Cinnamon covered, triangular pastries filled with sweet red bean paste.
7. Glutinous rice balls.
8. Literally 'pure water temple', this is one of Kyoto's most famous temples.
9. Kyoto's geisha district.

27. Journal

1. Japanese equivalent of Play-Doh.

29. Pokhara and the Sanctuary

1. Nepalese black tea boiled with condensed milk and sugar. Sickly sweet, but a great energy boost for weary trekkers.

30. Bedside Manner

1. Breakfast.
2. I don't understand. A very handy word to learn on the first day in Japan.
3. An honorific term for teacher, mentor, doctor.

31. No Baby

1. Please wait a moment.

36. Degree, Visa, Job — Check

1. English conversation.

39. Journal

1. Pronounced sar-kay. Popular Japanese whisky.

45. Parental Visit

1. Octopus.
2. Japanese style chopsticks pointed on the end and much easier to use than the Chinese variety.

50. Birthing Pool

1. An alternative birth method where the baby and placenta remain tethered until the cord withers and detaches by itself.

53. Spokeswoman

1. Bicycle shop.

54. Can I Borrow Your Washing Machine?

1. "Is that right?"
2. Good morning!
3. Washing machine.

61. The Final Chapter

1. Goodbye.

ACKNOWLEDGMENTS

Once again, there are so many people who contributed to the writing of *Gaijin,* either knowingly or unknowingly, and I am forever grateful for their input and sage advice.

To Iain, my love, for his endless patience and support.

To James, Mani and Noa, who lived the adventures with me, and made this book real.

To Joanna Chalmers, my fearless editor, for keeping me honest.

To my support team and early readers for your valued input.

And to all those who wandered in and out of my life in Japan and never dreamed they would end up mentioned in the pages of a book. The names may have been changed, but the details of our friendship live forever in my memory.

Thank you especially to my daughter, Noa, for her tireless editing and design work.

I love you and Mani to the moon and back.

ABOUT THE AUTHOR

Heather is not just an author. She is also a poet, a traveller, a photographer, a musician, an adventurer, a thrill seeker, a wife and a mother. She wears all these hats with confidence and style and brings her entire self to everything she does.

She has cycled across entire countries, camped under freeways, trekked the Himalaya with a baby on her back, lived in a bamboo hut on a Thai beach, worked as a cleaner in a motel, taught English to the Japanese, and been executive assistant to a Deputy Prime Minister of Australia. There's nothing she can't do or won't try. If she doesn't know, she makes it her mission to find out.

Heather currently lives on the Mid North Coast of New South Wales, Australia with her partner, Iain.

Gaijin Live Next Door is her second memoir.

https://www.heatherjhackett.com

facebook.com/heatherhackett.author
twitter.com/heatherhackett7
instagram.com/restless_travel_memoir

ALSO BY HEATHER HACKETT

Available from Amazon - https://www.amazon.com/dp/B01MXSWC3J/

Available for FREE download on my website -
https://www.heatherjhackett.com/restless-free-photo-book/

www.ingramcontent.com/pod-product-compliance
Lightning Source LLC
Chambersburg PA
CBHW020318010526
44107CB00054B/1886